Beyond the Curve of Spee
Surviving 4 years of Dental School

A Novel by Dr Ken Spaldane

Eloquent Books

Eloquent Books
An imprint of Strategic Book Group
P.O. Box 333
Durham CT 06422
www.StrategicBookGroup.com

ISBN 978-1-60860-290-2

Printed in the United States of America

Book Design/Layout by: Andrew Herzog

Dedication

I'd like to dedicate my novel to my wife, Nadine and my son, Grant.

FIRST YEAR

Looking around the room I wondered if I was in the wrong place. These students seemed more like the beautiful people of my high school's "IN" crowd than dental students. I had expected a lot of nerdy- intellectual types. Not the gorgeous ,curvaceous blonde a couple seats to my right or the buxom, expensively dressed dark haired beauty across the room. Most of the guys looked more like varsity all-star football players. I noticed only one really nerdy student with a buzz cut, wire-framed glasses and preppy attire. Radar ,from MASH , instantly came to mind.

I checked the room number on the door with the room number on my schedule. Room 203, yup, I was in the right place. Gross Anatomy Lab. The dank, dusty smell of formaldehyde agreed. This was gross.

At eight thirty sharp our instructor had his assistant close the door to the lab. We were trapped, committed. We were about to learn what the gross in gross anatomy meant.

"Welcome class, my name is Doctor Boch and I will be your instructor for gross anatomy 101. I will also be your instructor for dental anatomy 101 and oral histology 101. I expect full attendance at all of my classes and labs and I will not allow late comers." As if on cue there was a knock on the door. Dr Boch's assistant opened the door and three more students sheepishly entered the room. Dr Boch continued,"and those were the last three questions on your final exam". The late arrivals looked shell-shocked. Dr Bach laughingly admitted, "Just kidding, but seriously, to you people who just walked in I want you to know I will not tolerate any latecomers to my classes.

Now class without further ado I will show you what Gross Anatomy 101 is all about." -Dr Boch motioned to his assistant and together they rolled a large stainless steel vat on wheels into the center of the room. Dr Boch was short and Sicilian swarthy but pleasantly handsome. His assistant was a tall thin caricature of Ichabod Crane. His name tag said"-Wayne".

Together they rolled back the stainless steel lid to the nearest vat and the room instantly reeked of formaldehyde. The vat was filled with it. Dr Boch reached in with a rubber-gloved hand and brought pieces out of the liquid for our inspection. There were arms, legs, an upper torso sawn off at the waist and even a bodiless head. I almost lost my breakfast when he pulled the head out by its hair. Dripping formaldehyde the lifeless eyes stared out at us, the whole head swinging slowly to the right, then slowly to the left, taking us all in with its smoky gaze. One girl asked to be excused and had to leave the room. Ironically Dr Bach turned out to be one of our more caring and compassionate instructors. He was just a little warped.

After the welcoming display of various body parts we were ushered into an adjoining room to be introduced to our cadavers. Everyone was conspicuously silent. The inert bodies of our cadavers lay supine, zipped up in heavy -duty white vinyl bags, placed on top of stainless steel carts. We the living were divided into groups of four and each quartet had their own cadaver. Not really our own because we shared the same bodies with medical and physiotherapy students. The physios used the arms and legs, we used the head and neck and the med students got the rest. It seemed an equitable distribution though I worried about the med students. Where would they learn their head and neck anatomy? As we were assigned to our cadavers we split up and stood uneasily in our little groups beside our respective dead. I was with two guys and a girl. The girl had a face that resembled an inflated puffer fish. Heavy makeup couldn't cover the sporadic acne smeared around her cheeks and chin. If she lost the acne and about 30 psi she wouldn't be bad looking. One of the guys looked like a California surfer dude. He was at least 6 feet tall, with a dark tan and thick blonde hair ,that showed no sign of receding

The other guy resembled a cornered rat. He was of average height and build with short dark hair and vaguely Italian features. His eyes were working overtime, warily, sneakingly glancing around, being sure to avoid eye contact with anyone.

I felt like I had entered Dr Frankenstein's secret laboratory. The whole setting was too damn unnatural. I wanted to laugh or giggle,-anything to break the tension that was building. When Dr Boch told us to unzip the bags I was certain it was all a gag. Dr Boch had actually put live people in the bags and as soon as we unzipped them they'd all simultaneously open their eyes ,sit up and yell boo. Then we could all have a good laugh.

The four of us looked at each other except for the rodent guy who looked at the girl's boobs out of the corner of his eyes. The surfer guy introduced himself as Tom and asked," -Well who wants to do the honors?"We could hear the sounds of zippers being pulled down all around us and I was surprised when the girl volunteered. As we the living finished our introductions,

Amanda slowly unzipped our corpse. The zipper sounded like a long drawn out fart as it descended. I felt an overpowering urge to giggle. I could see the white waxy forehead and bloated chest through the unzipped but still mostly closed bag.

As Amanda pulled back the vinyl, our cadaver was displayed in all his deathly grandeur. There was no doubt as to his gender. His penis stretched between his legs like a snake. Although completely flaccid it must have been almost a foot long. As for the rest of his body he was about six feet tall and two hundred and fifty pounds. His diagnosis was death from congestive heart failure at age sixty-five.

Out of the corner of my eye I saw Dr Boch smiling like a retarded Cheshire cat. A couple of students from across the room started giggling. Dr Boch's grin faded. He cleared his throat and started into another speech -"I will not tolerate any form of disrespect for these cadavers. They have all selflessly donated their bodies to a good cause and I expect you to act with dignity and respect at all times. Is that clear?"

My urge to giggle intensified as I imagined slicing a scalpel through the dead flesh with my pinky finger extended. Suppressing the urge I studied our corpse. His color ranged from a pallid yellowish white to a purplish blue. Mostly he was just fat. Layers and layers of subcutaneous fat. There was going to have to be lots of cutting to get to any anatomically significant areas.

On instruction we zipped our cadavers back up and were herded into yet another room where we endured a two-hour introductory gross anatomy lecture.

In between gross anatomy and our next lecture we had an hour to check in with Dental Stores and receive our locker assignments and our student dental kits. Our student kits had cost us another $3500 each on top of our tuition. The kit included a low-speed and high-speed dental drill ,two articulators, each worth about $800 and assorted other dental instruments.

Our lockers were on the lowest level of the dental sciences building along with the first year dental lab for dental occlusion and restorative dentistry.-With no windows on this level it was possible to go a whole day without seeing the sun. The lack of windows and the subterranean locale of our classes and labs gave the place a very claustrophobic and vaguely sinister atmosphere.

The man behind the counter at dental stores was in a good mood. Quietly, and efficiently he was handing out our student kits, but he was also sizing us up, categorizing us already. He wore a long white lab coat over regular street clothes and over the pocket of his lab coat his name, RON, was sewn in blue thread.

I didn't know it then but Ron would eventually become the only real friend I had amongst the faculty. Although he was the dental storekeeper and not a professor or instructor, Ron usually knew more about what was going on within the faculty than anyone else. He always seemed to be the first to know if a new faculty appointment had been made or if a student was getting kicked out. I don't know how or where he got his information but Ron always had a finger on the pulse of the dental school.

The next lecture we had that first day was community dentistry. The head honcho, the big enchilada, The DEAN of the Faculty of dentistry actually welcomed us to Dentistry. His lecture was quite memorable. He said there would be two real high points in our four years of dental school- the day we were accepted and the day we walked across the graduation stage with our degrees. He warned us that dental school would be hard work and that acceptance did not guarantee graduation. He spoke of the high ethical standards expected from us and how we were all now representatives of his faculty.

As an example of these standards he mentioned how two years earlier a couple of dental students had been expelled from the faculty for cheating on an exam. One of them had been the class president. It was obvious,-after a while, that this professor liked to talk. Furthermore he liked to use as many big words as possible. He described dentistry as a dynamic, multifocal-egregious profession.

That day he also told us that somewhere in the lecture room there was another dental student who we probably didn't know yet who would stand as our best man/bridesmaid someday.

Despite his propensity for using multi-syllabic words he seemed to exude a general feeling of welcome and warmth. We all left the lecture feeling a little inflated.

It didn't take long to deflate us. Our next class after lunch was the soon to be dreaded dental occlusion . The class was three hours long. For the first hour we heard the drill seargent Dr Moore, lecture and quiz us. The next two hours of the class were spent waxing up teeth. Dr

Moore had a seating plan in front of him with everyone's picture. He warned us that by the end of the year he would know every one of us personally.

His comments reminded me of what my family dentist had cautioned me of when I told him I'd been accepted. He warned me that the best way to survive dental school was to keep a low profile and that it was best to be average. If you either failed or excelled you would draw yourself to notoriety. Supposedly if you could walk across the stage at graduation and have the majority of professors not know who you were, you'd have succeeded admirably. And Dr Moore wanted to break the security of anonymity already on the first day of first year.

Great!!

For dental occlusion 101 we started by waxing up the maxillary,(upper) right central incisor. Next we would do the lateral incisor, the canine-the two premolars and then we would end with the molars. The waxing up exercise would help develop our manual dexterity as well as familiarize ourselves with the shape, contours and dimensions of the teeth. Each week we were marked on our wax-up efforts.

It was in this class that most of us were first introduced to sadistic and cruel instructors .

The class was divided into four rows. Each row had a separate instructor who was responsible for marking us. I was in B-row and my instructor was Dr Rabst. He was a tall, thin bespectacled, slightly balding, typical looking dentist in his early forties. Although he looked fairly benevolent, in retrospect I think he was an honorary SS member. Yet compared to some of the instructors I was still to meet, he was a mere babe in arms.

Dr Rabst told us openly that he liked to make things stressful so we would be prepared for the clinic and eventually private practice. At least he was honest.

It was important to get a good start on the wax-up because at the end of next class our efforts

would be marked. We used bunsen burners to heat up a red colored wax that we blobbed onto a root stump that would eventually through our efforts develop into a tooth. By successive additions of melted wax we'd build up an amorphous mass that could be carved to the proper size and shape. Our final wax-ups were only slightly bigger than normal teeth in size.

When the hot wax dropped accidentally on your skin it was painful. That first afternoon I must have burned myself either with the hot instruments or the hot wax at least a half dozen times. They were only the first of countless self-inflicted injuries I would sustain in the next four years .

By the end of class my central incisor still looked like a big blob of wax,only distantly resembling a tooth. In the interests of paranoia we were told to lock up our waxing efforts at the back of the room in cupboards which only Dr Moore had the key to.

We would only be allowed to wax-up during regular class time. This way-at least Dr Moore said, they could determine right from the start who was having difficulties. I could see that Tuesday afternoons were going to be fun. At my locker I couldn't get my lock to unlock. In frustration I went and sat down in one of the cubicles, in the adjoining washroom. I felt like crying. To calm myself down I mentally reflected on the events of the preceeding few months, since I found out I had been accepted to dental school.

It had all started with a phone call.

My sister's voice sounded strained so I knew something was up. She began with "-A letter came for you today from the university. It has 'personal and confidential' , stamped across the front." My heart started racing -"Open it.-" I stammered. There was a long pause and I knew she was reading the letter first. I remember thinking to myself "Please, please let this be it". My impatience got the best of me and I practically yelled into the phone, "What is it? What does it say?" In reply she started reading in a flat -emotionless, sibling rivalry tone of voice, "Dear Mr

Ken Spaldane : We are pleased to inform you that you have been accepted into the first year at the Faculty of Dentistry for the academic year 1983/1984."

My sister kept on reading but I couldn't really assimilate what she was saying. I couldn't believe it. I was In!!! I'd made it!!

I was so excited I spent the rest of that day in a kind of haze. I played co-ed softball that evening and I felt unstoppable, undefeatable. I hit three home runs and made incredible diving catches.

It wasn't until a week or so later that the reality of the acceptance slowly changed my euphoria into a lower level of smug joy. I realized I'd have to find a place to live in a totally new city. Soon I'd be in a classroom with 51 other students and initially wouldn't know any of them. The prospect of so much change seemed intimidating. I wondered how hard the courses would be and I even felt some uncertainty and fear that I might not make it.

By the middle of July I'd found a place to live. The university was in a moderate sized city about eighty miles west of the city I had grown up in. A friend of mine from high school, Mark,- was taking a Master's degree in urban planning at the University and he was conveniently in need of a new roommate. Mark had rented a house with three other students and they needed a fourth. The house was only about two miles from the University and since I had no other leads I decided to join them.

I knew Mark worked hard at his studies and took school seriously. He reassured me that the other roommates were hard workers and serious students as well, There was John in 4th year honors math,Tim in 3rd year mechanical engineering, and George in the 3rd year of a general math program. I figured you wouldn't have reached the 3rdor 4th year of a university program unless you had good study habits and a quiet home environment. In the year I spent there I never saw one of them crack a book-,ever. I had the only bedroom on the first floor. My room was adjacent to the living room, and every night they stayed up late watching David Letterman. Not one of them had classes before noon. Another thing they didn't tell me was that they were all on academic probation because of their involvement in theft for under $500. The house was decorated with street signs that had been cunningly removed from around the city over the previous three years. A sympathetic judge let them off with 60 hours of community service and academic probation. And actually George was spending his 7th academic year hoping he might have enough credits to get a three-year degree in ANYTHING.

I learned fairly early on that I wasn't going to be able to study at the house and that I was not going to get any sympathy from my roommates.

After I paid my $250 deposit to hold my place in the first year class they sent me information that included an orientation schedule, a list of required and recommended textbooks and a timetable .The timetable looked bleak. -8:30 to 5:00 pm five days a week, with only an hour off for lunch and no other breaks. Nine different courses. In my undergraduate years I was usually able to avoid early morning classes and my timetable had been more like Swiss cheese with an hour or two off after most classes. Eight thirty to five sounded too much like a real job. I wondered when I would have time to study.

I moved into the house a week before classes started. That day I toured the campus and dental sciences building and I bought most of my textbooks at the university bookstore. The house was still deserted when I moved in with my clothes, books, stereo, futon and everything else I needed to make the room feel like home. My room was large but it had some definite negative qualities. It was beside the living room and the kitchen and the nearest washroom was upstairs. Mark had told me that the other guys wouldn't be moving in until after the long weekend.

⁎ ⁎ ⁎

But now summer was over and I was sitting in a washroom, beaten by a two-dollar combination lock. How the hell was I going to make it through four years of dental school if I couldn't conquer a lousy combination lock ? I left the washroom, walked down the hallway and went to try again.

When I got home that night in a decidedly foul mood my roommates were sprawled out on the dilapidated student couches in the living room. They were working through a two-four of Miller and planning their strategy for the year. Not wanting to be antisocial I joined them for a couple beers. Apparently their collective strategy for the year was to party Thursday, Friday and Saturday, rest on Sunday and study from Monday to Wednesday. Of course George never studied. He just partied 24/7. George reminded me of the middle son from Eight is Enough. He had curly blond hair, a medium build and a winning smile. In high school he had been captain of his football team. Unfortunately his high school was so far in the boonies of his state that they probably would have given full scholarships to Daryl, Daryl and Daryl .He was hopeful that he would be able to graduate after this last (his 7th) year of university.

John looked like someone you didn't mess around with. He had a majorly receding hairline and an extensive bushy moustache that drew attention away from his head. Although John was of medium build and height he seemed bigger. Maybe it was the almost hypnotic way he had of looking at you with his slate blue eyes. John made no bones about wanting to be fabulously wealthy someday. His honors math degree would hopefully get him started on that road to riches.

Tim was tall, good looking and always had perfect hair. He was the unofficial and undisputed boss of the house. Being arrogant and self-centered he had as many enemies as friends. Mark,my friend from high school,also wanted to be wealthy one day. He was hoping to get into commercial real estate. Mark was very good looking,-needless to say he was popular with the ladies

The other important strategies they were planning that evening had to do with the pursuit and picking up of women. Apparently the first few weeks of school were crucial because it was then that young, naive, highly impressionable women were the most available. As the school year progressed these types slowly went out of circulation as they became involved and subsequently lost their vulnerability. Naive, gorgeous young women were their specialty. Over the year I knew I would be entertained by their varying degrees of success. When the beer was finished they all went to the student pub and I went to my room to start on my reading. In one day I'd been assigned over eighty pages to read and assimilate. Sixty pages for dental occlusion and over 25 pages for gross anatomy. It was difficult to concentrate and I'd only gotten through about ten pages of gross anatomy when I fell asleep. My roommates made so much noise when they got back from the pub that I woke up and couldn't get back to sleep. Instead of tossing and turning in bed I got up and watched David Letterman with them.

It gave me a chance to get to know them better. As I sat there I felt like an outsider. Tim was talking about the pub they were at. "What a waste of time. There were hardly any chicks there, and the ones that were there-,were dogs,- he exclaimed. Gord put his two cents in. " I remember four years ago, when all the pubs were filled with babes. It was like falling off a log. You couldn't miss. Chicks are way too uptight these days-They want to know what your major is, what your dad does and if you have money. It's bullshit!"

I ventured my opinion."Maybe it's a bad year for chicks," I said. My comment was met by a stony silence. All eyes were suddenly intent on the television screen. I felt like yelling. "What have I done wrong? Why don't you guys like me? What is the fricking problem, you assholes?" Instead I sat there feeling more and more alone. I tried again, "-Tough room -" More silence.

I hoped that things would get better as the year went by.

The next day was largely a didactic or lecture day. I found it rough getting up at seven since I'd only slept about five hours. That morning I almost fell asleep in both biochemistry and histology. Both classes were exceedingly dull. Luckily biochemistry was going to be easy since the course content was almost identical to the introductory biochemistry I'd taken two years previously as a chemistry undergraduate.

I wish I could say the same thing about histology. Histology is the department of anatomy that deals with the minute or microscopic structure, composition and function of living tissues. For many of the students histology was just review, but for me it was all new.

I felt totally lost with terms like endoplasmic reticulum and mitochondria. I had to review basic cell structure and function just to understand the lectures.

After lunch we had our first physiology lecture. This was a course that we took with the medical students. The lecture room was almost filled to capacity with 120 of them and just 52 of us. Luckily for me I'd taken a very basic human physiology course a year before. If it wasn't for that I would have been lost.

Our lecturer was a short Pakistani doctor who talked exceedingly fast while writing on the chalkboard with his right hand and simultaneously erasing with his left hand -By the end of the class my head was reeling with facts and theories and my hand was cramped from writing so much. To top it off we received yet another reading assignment. Two chapters from the monolithic Medical Physiology text. We ended the day with another lecture in histology.

At home I fell asleep for a couple hours while trying to read physiology. I'd cracked the book open at five..... next thing I knew it was seven and I was still on page four. Futons and physiology were a potent sedative.

That night I did more reading and memorized my schedule for the year. Basically the academic year was divided into four quarters. Each quarter was eight weeks long and at the end of each quarter we had exams. That meant four sets of exams a year. The schedule was changed slightly with each new quarter. Some classes lasted all year while others only went until Christmas.

Thursday morning was reserved for operative dentistry. Operative dentistry was basically just,"drill and fill".As the bread and butter of dentistry it was a monumentally important subject. Our morning started with a one-hour introductory lecture and then for the rest of the morning they let us play with our drills. We drilled plastic replicas of normal sized teeth, mounted in an artificial mouth-,known as a dentoform. It would take two full years of practicing on these plastic teeth before we would be allowed near a live patient with our drills. Good thing too!

Our lecturer, Dr Willis-, was very matter-of-fact."There is no room for error in operative dentistry," he exclaimed."Some of you may never develop the skills needed to be a good dentist and in this course we will find you, we will weed you out." I looked around the room and wondered who the weeds were. Most of the students were busy looking at their own shoes or the walls, being careful to avoid eye contact with Dr Willis. He sounded too damn eager to do some weeding.

Dr Willis was a tall, gangly, almost completely bald man with a full beard. He exuded confidence, arrogance and cruelty.-Apparently Dr Willis had been through a particularly onerous divorce. He had previously collected corvettes but now that his ex-wife and lawyer had his two favorites, he was looking for a new hobby. At times Dr Willis was helpful and caring but at other times he was harsh and intimidating. In general he was someone to stay away from.

Dr Willis also liked to play favorites. Each year he would choose two or three students he felt were particularly talented with their hands and he would encourage and even pamper them every step of the way. At the other end of the spectrum he'd find a few students he felt were the worst and he'd ride them all year long.

Evaluation in operative dentistry was based on written exams-(fifteen percent),drilling and filling assignments-(twenty-five percent) and four dreaded practical exams-(sixty percent). To pass you needed a minimum of sixty percent in both the didactive and practical components. The practical exams were probably the most stressful of all experiences in dental school. At least our first practical exam wasn't for another eight weeks.

That afternoon we had an introductory lecture in oral medicine and afterwards we were given a tour of the main student dental clinic, During the lecture we learned that the sum total of all clinical experiences in first year consisted of looking at one another's teeth . If we wanted more clinical experience we could go and watch(hold suction for) our third and fourth year classmates anytime we had free time. (Right!)

As we were led on our first tour of the clinic I couldn't help but be impressed. There were over a hundred separate cubicles, each equipped with its own dental chair-The cubicles walls were a uniform four and a half feet tall across the whole clinic floor.

There were no windows on this level but the fluorescent lighting seemed to simulate daylight. Maybe it was just the enormity of the clinic that gave it that bright, open impression. Unfortunately the color scheme was stuck in the late seventies. The walls were avocado green and the dental chairs were harvest gold.

As we were led through the clinic, meek as the mice in the Pied Piper, we witnessed a disturbing scene.

The third and fourth year students were working on patients at the time of our tour. Above the general din of the clinic we heard an old man's hysterical sounding voice. "I want to kill myself, I'm going to kill myself." The man's voice wavered in tone but increased in volume. Our instructor led us in the opposite direction of the fracas, fast. Despite the attempt at damage control most of us saw the cause of the disturbance. "Now, now, everything's going to be alright. Don't worry, the denture is going to be fine" The professor was trying to calm the half-sobbing pale,-old man sitting in the dental cubicle. Further back in the same cubicle was a student who looked both disgusted and afraid. He was picking up what looked to be a broken denture off the floor. The old man had settled into a mantra. "I'm going to kill myself, I want to kill myself."

By the time we had reached the other end of the clinic the drama was over. But it was too late. The freeze-frame moment of strangeness was indelibly etched in my mind. We never did learn what happened or even what the whole scene was about.

* * *

That night we had our first official Dentistry Pub. By the evening of the pub our class had already started dividing into groups and cliques. It was a sort of a polarization of like-mindedness. Keener types who sat in the front row and liked to answer questions recognized others of their sub-genre and started to hang together. Preppy types who wore alligator shirts, Bermuda shorts and loafers compared fashion notes. Quiet people kept with quiet people and loud people got together with other loud people trying to outdo each other. Friendships were being made that would last a lifetime. But the real polarization into two distinct groups would take time. The difference between the two groups would probably best be illustrated by their response to a simple question. "What do you think of dental school? " If your response was, "It sucks" you were one of us-the normal people. The other type of student in response to the same question would say something like, "I think it's great." while staring at a spot somewhere over your left shoulder in the vicinity of Pluto. For some reason the second group never seemed to have problems with our instructors. I guess they were on the same wavelength.

I went to the first Dents Pub with Dan. I had sat beside Dan during a lot of the classes and he'd kept me awake with his whispered side cracks. He seemed to have a low opinion of most of our instructors and the crap they were feeding us. Ironically he would become a top student. Yet he never did lose that disdain for the instructors or the system. I think that's why we got along so well.

Although Dan dressed like a preppy he had come from a low-income working class family in Hamilton. He'd made his way through university by working like a dog and grabbing whatever scholarships he could along the way. Dan was five feet three inches tall. He had short, always perfectly groomed Ken Doll blonde hair and the bluest eyes I'd ever seen. His wire-rimmed glasses and short stature earned him the nickname "Radar" amongst the majority of our class.

* * *

Dan didn't give a shit. He couldn't care less what people called him.

That night our mission was to get laid. We arrived in style in Dan's 1962 white MGB Roadster. He'd bought it for $500 a couple of years ago and had restored it completely with the help of his father who was an auto body mechanic. Driving up to the pub I noticed we got a few looks. Unfortunately that was all we got that night. I looked like the boy next door. Since my dad was Finn and my mother Ukrainian my overall features were slightly Slavic. I was in good shape and had almost no body fat. I was average in height but I had a forty-six inch chest and thirty two inch waist. I was twenty-two years old and my blonde hair was just starting to recede. I was very self-conscious about my hairline. I had gone into Co-op Chemistry right after I graduated from grade thirteen. My marks weren't that great in high school so I really thought I was going to be a chemist. Just before I was ready to start chemistry I had a life-changing experience. I was at a Junior Forest Ranger camp for the summer and there had been a hor-rible accident. Two of my best friends burned to death in a controlled forest fire gone bad. By a twist of fate I ended up on a canoe trip instead of going to the fire. Our foreman decided to take me on a whim, otherwise I would have been dead, burned to death. When they found the bodies their yellow hard hats had melted to their heads.

At that point faced with my own mortality I decided I was going to make my life count for something. When I started university I applied myself like I never had before. My first term marks were all in the mid-eighties to nineties. At that point I started thinking seriously about wanting to be a dentist. I had always liked working with my hands. My mother told me that if she ever had a knot in sewing she just gave it to me. Even as a young child I had the skill and patience to undo even her worst knots. The other things about dentistry that appealed to me were being my own boss and having the prestige of being called a doctor. In high school my marks weren't high enough so I never really took the idea of being a dentist seriously. But now that I was getting good marks it seemed a real possibility.

I waited until I had three years of Chemistry under my belt before I applied to dentistry. The odds of getting accepted were not good. Of the two thousand students who applied to dental school each year in our state, only one hundred and sixty were accepted.

For the acceptance process they looked at three things-your marks, your score on the DAT (Dental Aptitude Test), and a personal interview. The cut-off point was eighty one percent and I needed to score higher than average on all aspects of the DAT.

I did the DAT in December just before Christmas, in my third year of Chemistry. In total there were about two hundred hopefuls on that cold, blustery day. The DAT was a full day exam and consisted of three distinct components. First we had to carve a piece of chalk to very specific dimensions. Next was a reading comprehension component and finally there was a test on three-dimensional problem solving.

We started with the chalk carving first. We all sat down and at the appointed time we were to pick up the directions for carving and the piece of chalk. The guy beside me had a problem. When he picked up his directions the piece of chalk that was inside, rolled very slowly in the direction of the edge of the table. We both watched the slow motion roll that sent the chalk off the edge of the table only to have it break into two pieces when it hit the floor. He was dark skinned and looked very Arab. He spoke with a Middle Eastern accent. He called one of the proctors over. "I have had problem, look at my chalk,- it is no good, I need another piece," he cried. The proctor looked like he was going to start laughing. "I' m sorry, we can't give you another piece of chalk, you're just going to have to make do with what you have." "No, this can't be true, I have given up my dancing for this. It is not my fault. The chalk broke before I touched it,"he cried again. The proctor definitely looked amused. "I'm sorry-those are the rules." He exclaimed. The hapless victim continued, "But you don't understand. I have given up my DANCING for this. You can not do this to me!" The proctor ignored him and walked away. "But I have given up my dancing," he implored me. Tough luck, buddy, I thought. The chalk carving was brutal. I had practiced for hours with kid's street chalk, but this chalk had a totally different feel. It was so soft that you could almost cut it with a thought. I didn't take chances. I carved as slowly and carefully as possible. The only problem was that I ran out of time. I had finished about ninety percent, so when we were asked to put our chalk down I was a little depressed. I looked over to my swarthy buddy and felt a lot better.

The reading comprehension was a scientific paper on sediment rates in river deltas. It was so full of technical details that the article was virtually impossible to understand. I answered the questions as well as I could, but by the time I was finished I felt totally frazzled.

The last part of the test went as well as could be expected. I had a natural knack for visualizing in three dimensions so I think I did fairly well. As I got ready to leave, I looked around the room and wondered which of us, if any, would become dentists. I thought my swarthy buddy should have stuck to his dancing.

When I got the results in March I was pleasantly surprised. I had scored above average on all three parts of the test and I was even in the top one percentile for the three dimensional problem-solving component.

That night Dan and I got to know each other better, but we didn't pick up any girls.

After waiting in line for about an hour and seeing that we were going nowhere fast, despite having tickets we returned to the Roadster and roared away to another student pub at the university. The ratio of guys to girls was about ten to one. We waited in yet another line for about twenty minutes before we got in.

After a couple beers I asked a girl to dance. She turned me down without even glancing at me.After my rejection Dan didn't even bother trying. We had a couple more beers and called it a night. So much for getting laid.

Friday was another lecture day. Biochemistry, histology and physiology. The only new class was DMS or dental materials science. It was the last class on Friday afternoon and it was a sleeper, The lecturer, Dr Taurn, was actually a nice man,-(rare in the dental faculty-)but he didn't know the first thing about lecturing. He started and ended each sentence with an, "Uh" although I'm not sure he ever managed to put together a complete sentence. Ever.

That first introductory lecture he put graph after graph and phase diagram after phase diagram on an overhead screen and he managed to confuse even the brightest of us, not to mention himself. It was pointless to ask questions since his standard response went something like, "Uh, don't uh worry,- you uh don't (sniff) have to (cough) know this for your uh, uh,- exam."

It was during this class that I had a very embarrassing moment. Right in the middle of one of

Dr Taurn's exhaustive monologues I had the urge to sneeze. When the sneeze came I stifled it by closing my nose with my fingers. Unfortunately I didn't stifle the loud, resonating liquid fart that came out instead.- I must have turned bright red and it seemed like the entire class was roaring with laughter. If it had happened in third or fourth year it wouldn't have been such a big deal. Of course by that time I would have probably received a standing ovation. Feeling quite ashamed, I couldn't wait for the class to be over.

* * *

My whole life I never felt like I fit in anywhere. Not with my family, not in high school and certainly not in dental school. My parents had a normal middle class existence. My father worked as a night editor for our local paper and my mother was an elementary school teacher. I had three sisters and no brothers. I was the third oldest. Growing up I had no interest in sports because my dad had no interest in sports. When I started school I had a severe speech impediment. I wasn't able to say the "Arrrr...." sound at all. Instead of saying Karl I had to get by with Kawel. Which made life difficult for me because my parents named me Karl Kenneth Spaldane. I insisted that everyone call me Ken, so I unofficially, officially became Ken Spaldane.

My mother had a friend who was a speech therapist and she agreed to tutor me for free. I had the feeling that if my parents would have had to pay out of their own pockets I'd still be introducing myself as Kawel. I remember repeating again and again.- "The bird sat on the board". Except for me it came out. "The beux-d sat on the boad." My little sister,who was two years younger than I sang merrily, "The bird sat on the board" with absolutely crystal clear pronunciation. My sister Susan,who was one year older than I, hated my guts. I had skipped a year in grade three putting us in the same grade and even the same classes in high school. To make matters worse I always got higher marks then she did. In our grade eleven yearbook our pictures were right beside each other.

Her cut line read," -No relation." When I was accepted to study chemistry she knew she had to one-up me.

She applied for and was accepted to Chemical Engineering. Like me, she was in a cooperative program. The program gave us a full two years of work experience as well as an honors degree.

She came across so poorly in her interviews that she only had one real engineering job. For the other work terms she ended up working at donut shops or variety stores. During her one real engineering job she was the only female at her job site. For a joke her fellow workers tied her up and put her into a large card-board box that was stamped, "Special delivery, fragile." It was addressed to a factory in China. With some effort she was able to free herself and walked out of the building,- never to go back. When I was accepted to study dentistry I thought she was going to implode with jealousy. All through dental school I kept getting special packages and letters that I had to pick up at the post office. I always got excited because I never knew who the mail was from. All of the correspondences came from her. They all had the same content. " I hate you, I hate you,I hate you." I had to admire her persistence. One letter I found particularly amusing. It read,"You probably don't remember this but when you were four and I was five you stole my wagon in the sand box. I can never forgive you for that. That was the exact moment that I began my downward spiral in life." She averaged about two thousand words per correspondence and it was obvious that she had put a lot of thought into her efforts. I always had the feeling that she was my dad's favorite. When we were quite young (- I think I was in grade two-) my dad read us the story of "Jonathon Livingston Seagull." Afterwards he asked us questions. He was quite excited and we all wanted to see him pleased with our responses. My dad got more and more disappointed and eventually a little upset because none of us had any idea what the book was about. Except for Susan. She at least understood that the book wasn't just about seagulls. Besides not feeling like I fit in any-where I also had problems with self-esteem. I never felt like I was good enough and I always felt like I could do better. If I had ninety-eight on an exam I would proudly announce the mark to my parents. My dad's response was always the same. "Did any one get a higher mark?" I always had to confess, "Yeah, Dad, Todd Wilfong got ninety-nine percent." It didn't matter what I achieved,-my parents always had to break my bubble.

Getting high marks in Co-op Chemistry helped with my self-esteem problem. I was accepted to study dentistry largely because of my eighty-five percent accumulative average from chemistry. In total I ended up with two whole years of job experience learning to be a chemist. It was largely through these jobs that I decided chemistry was not going to be my destiny. The jobs were either low paying or incredibly dull, or both.

My first job was working at a soap plant,- owned by a large multinational. They manufactured different brands of soap including Zest. My job was to run quality control tests on the soaps to make sure that they were made according to specifications. I was even given my own research project. I was to test three different bleaching agents to make soap lighter in color. Everything went well with the lab tests. Hydrogen peroxide came out as the winner with a thirty percent increase in brightness.

I was given permission to run a plant scale test on a Sunday. I slowly added the hundred gallons of hydrogen peroxide to the humongous five-ton vat of liquid soap. I watched in horror as the soap level started to rise. It kept rising and rising until the soap was frothing over the edge of the vat. It just kept coming and coming until there was almost no soap left in the original vat.

I was devastated. I thought for sure that when I arrived for work on Monday that I was going to be fired. That Monday I made sure I was at work at least fifteen minutes early. My boss Ernie walked into his office about ten minutes later. Ernie,-the Worm, as he was known throughout the plant, came out of his office about fifteen minutes later and made a bee line for me. He was called the Worm because he always weaseled his way out of trouble by kissing the asses of his superiors. He never took blame for anything and somehow he had survived as plant manager for almost twenty years.

" Ken, come on into my office, I hear you had a little excitement this weekend," he said humorously. I replied. "Sir I am so sorry, I don't know what happened. Everything was fine in the lab test, but yesterday was a total disaster.The soap went everywhere. I was practically in tears as I saw my job going out the window. The Worm put his arm around my shoulder, and speaking as if I was his son, said, "You know,twenty-five years ago I did the same thing as you, except that instead of five tons I did fifty- Don't worry, all the wasted soap is just being recycled, so there's no real harm done. Now Ken, breathe."

I left his office a grinning fool. My co-workers came up to me, curious to know my fate. "So what did the Worm do to you?"said their designated spokesman. I replied, still grinning, "Absolutely nothing!" "Oh man,- the Worm likes you,- you are so lucky."

My next work term left me at another branch of the same multinational. This time I was working at a meat packaging plant. My job was to do quality control tests on the various meat products that were made at the plant, like hot dogs, bologna and other lunch meats. After an extensive training course I was left running the lab from five in the afternoon to midnight. Nick was a frequent visitor to the lab. He used our super accurate weigh scales to measure his drugs. The whole time I knew him he was always high on something. He had come from Yugoslavia five years before and he couldn't believe the abundances of our society.

Nick's job was to add the additives to the various meat products as they were being made. This presented me with a moral dilemma. When we discovered in the lab that the hot dogs had accidentally double the required amount of salt we knew that Nick had forgotten he had already added salt to the mix and just added another batch. I never did rat on Nick because I really liked him. He used to come into the lab just to shoot the shit. " You know Ken, when I was in Yugoslavia I had nothing, you know-nothing. But I was happy. Women liked me,-"he started. "-But here I am a nobody, but that is why I sell my drugs. When I walk into a room at a party, now everyone comes up to me and says,'Nick,how are you? Nick, what is going on? Nick, what do you got?'And I am glad. Everybody likes me. But still here, I am not happy. I wish to go back to my old country, but then I will have nothing."

He used to always give me advice about women, but after hearing his stories about his conquests I found it hard to take him seriously, He told me about the woman who fell asleep on him in the middle of love making. And the two high school girls who tried to blackmail him afterwards.

Every night when I rode the streetcar back to my dive of an apartment I was followed by dogs. The smell of the hot dogs and other meats had permeated into my skin and I was apparently irresistible to them. After a while I started carrying dog treats in my pocket so I wouldn't get eaten.

My third work term landed me in a different city working for the leading steel-making plant in the country. My job was to test various lubrication fluids to make sure there were no irregularities. The lab I worked in was huge and there were well-established social cliques. As a student I was pretty well left to my own devices. There was a guy there named Norm who was the unofficial loser of the lab. While being in his mid-forties, he still lived at home with his mom. On holidays he used to drive around the country looking at trains.That was his hobby. Trainspotting. He had a bad habit of taking the eraser end of his pencil and digging in his ear with it. Afterwards he brought the eraser tip up to his nose and sniffed it. He always made sure no one was looking when he did it, when in fact half of us were covertly watching.

Norm used to drink tea,-and he brewed his tea in a big lab beaker over a bunsen burner. The guys in the lab got me to play a cruel joke on Norm. While his tea was bubbling over the flame they distracted him while I dropped a little phthenopthalein into his drink. Phthenopthalein is the active ingredient in Ex Lax. The next day Norm didn't show up for work. Or the next day after. Finally three days later he showed up for work looking haggard and tired. I don't think any of us expected such drastic results.

My next work term was at the same steel-making company but at a different lab. This lab was smaller and there were only five permanent workers and two students. The lab was the main research lab for the company and my job consisted of four months of drilling holes through steel plates. Three weeks before the official end of our jobs, all of the students were given pink slips. The company was struggling and the first to go were the student jobs.

My last job was at Sick Kids Hospital. Officially I was a student researcher but in reality I was a glorified gopher for a graduate student working on her Phd. I loved going down to the cafeteria in my long white lab coat and picture ID. I knew that people would think I was a real doctor, when I was actually just a student. In the research department there was a definite hierarchy. On top were the doctors who ran the labs. They were usually professors in the Faculty of Medicine at the nearby university. Next came the post-docs (students who had already earned their Phd's but were unable to get teaching jobs.) The post-docss did most of the actual research in the labs. They were the work-horses. Next came the graduate students who were trying to get their Master's or Phd's. And at the bottom of the barrel was anyone else. I was slightly above the cleaners and custodial staff.

My graduate student, Sara, was doing work on the myelin sheath on people who suffered from multiple sclerosis. She was hoping to understand better why the myelin sheath degraded in people with the disease.

Dr Marks who ran the lab was fantabulously wealthy. He had started up the first medical testing labs in the state and sold them when he was still a young man. He drove a top of the line Mercedes Benz and lived in a supposed mansion in the most exclusive area of town. I told him once when we were talking that I'd gotten a haircut. He said. "Which one? " The joke went right over my head and I just stood there like an idiot while he chuckled to himself.

Sara was very kind to me and never worked me very hard.I freaked out when I was told that I would have to sacrifice (kill) live rats. Sara showed me how to do it. She placed their little necks on the edge of a table top surface and by applied pressure while twisting, she killed them quickly and easily. I told Sara, " I can't kill them! I don't want to build up any more bad karma than I can help." She was cool. She replied, "No problem, don't worry about it. I'll take the karmic hit for you. I think I'm coming back as a grasshopper anyways." We both laughed.

Another gross part of the job was putting brains into blenders. In the freezers we had a ready supply of both cow and human brains. To isolate the myelin sheath from the rest of the brain,the first step was to actually cut up the brain and slip it into the blender for a two minute puree.

At this step the pureed brain had a very unique smell that was totally unlike anything else. It was sort of a peppery milky smell with an undertone of beef. They say that intelligence is dependant on the number of folds that are in the brain. I think we had the Einstein of cows because one particular cow brain had so many folds it almost looked like a human brain.

That weekend was the first of many wild times. My room-mates were definitely a bad influence. On Saturday night we had our first house party. There must have been over three hundred people crammed into our house. Add to that the people on the porch, lawn, neighbors lawn and street and in total there must have been at least five hundred partiers. It wasn't until two am that the party started to slow down a bit. I had spent most of my time talking with a voluptuous nursing student from Toronto. I was trying to get her alone in my bedroom. The only problem was that I couldn't get the fifty or so other people out of my bedroom. In frustration I just started kissing her anyways. She responded by kissing me back passionately. Ellen was a twenty-one,year-old. second year nursing student who had come down to visit her best friend who was taking nursing at our university. Her best friend knew my roommate John and in fact had dated him for a few years. Eventually people started to leave my room and finally I booted the last few stragglers out and locked the door. Ellen and I were alone at last. We lay down on my futon and fooled around until we were both exhausted. We fell fast asleep intertwined together like two little bear cubs. The next day we slept in until noon. I woke up with the odd sensation of being watched and sure enough when I opened my eyes Ellen was there staring right at me. "Do you know that you snore?" "Good morning, gorgeous," I rolled over and gave her a big morning-after kiss.-Gross. She didn't seem to mind. "So Ellen, feel like helping to clean this place up?" We ended up with over one hundred and twenty dollars in beer bottle returns,from that one party. Later that day I asked her if she was interested in going out together for a while. She seemed thrilled and we made plans for me to visit her in Toronto the next weekend. the long distance aspect was annoying but at least I would have time during the week for studying. That evening I finished all my reading assignments. I had survived my first whole week of dental school. I was three percent done first year and point eight three percent done all of dental school. Of course I had no idea of what still lay ahead. The next week was passing rather uneventfully until the next session of dental occlusion. During the lecture session Dr Moore,-went down the class list alphabetically and asked everyone a question. At least it was predictable because you knew when it was your time to answer. Dr Moore put a slide of a tooth up on the screen and asked, " Miss Martin, is this a view from the distal.(back) or mesial,(front) of the tooth? Mister Pinnel, what tooth is this? "And so it went. Next week Dr Moore would start asking us questions at random and he specialized in asking students who weren't paying attention or looked confused.

From then on we were forced to pay attention because we never knew when the question would come. That afternoon Dr Rabst marked our first wax-ups. He started at the far end of the row and worked his way like an advancing cobra up towards the front of the row where I sat. When he got to me he looked hungry. He picked up my wax-up, looked at it from every conceivable angle, took a deep breath and started, "Well,..., what do you think is wrong with this tooth?" It looked pretty good to me for my first effort and I told him so. From his reaction you'd think I'd told him I'd slept with his wife. " What," he whined indignantly. " What about this height of contour here?" He took his pen and dented in the side of the tooth. " How about this area here?

Don't you think it's a little bulbous? " He picked up my carver and ripped it across the front of the tooth. " As well, don't you think this edge is too thick?" He dug into the soft wax again. "How about the contact with the next tooth? Don't you think it's too heavy?"

If I agreed with him he criticized me and if I disagreed with him he got angry. I couldn't win. By the time he was finished my wax-up was massacred with scratches and dents and he looked like he was in a post-orgasmic resolution phase. He handed me my mark card, (sixty-three percent) and told me he wanted to see an improvement on my next effort. Afterwards, by comparing with others I found out I'd done not too badly. Some had much higher marks but most had marks in the sixties.

A handful had even failed. Right across from me in Row A, a fellow student,- Marcus, had been supremely lambasted by his row instructor. I noticed later when Marcus's instructor whispered something in Dr Moore's ear and pointed directly at the hapless Marcus. It looked like he was a marked man. On the next wax-up Dr Rabst said I'd improved,(sixty-seven percent),but I still had a long way to go. He'd only found three things with my wax-up that he could criticize. The third wax-up he failed me,(fifty-eight percent).He even took me aside and asked me if I really wanted to be a dentist. This did wonders for my self-confidence. I found out later that about a third of the class had similar discussions with their instructors.What did they honestly expect us to say? "Uh Gee, no I don't want to be a dentist. See you later. I'm going home to tell my family and friends that dentistry is not for me. Dr Rabst wanted to make us so angry that we'd have to do good wax-ups just to piss him off. After my failure I became more tense and worried and every Tuesday afternoon I'd develop a tension headache that turned into a throbbing, pulsing pain by five o'clock.

Oddly enough my carvings started to improve. I think he knew he'd pushed me to the edge and if he pushed me any further I might crack. So for my next wax-ups I got a sixty-nine percent, seventy- three percent and then a sixty-four percent. I was holding my own. Meanwhile Dr Rabst had made one girl in our class cry. Marcus, across from me should have cried with the pathetic progress he was making. He had failed every single wax-up. It became a vicarious pleasure to watch him get torn apart by his row instructor. I think it made us all feet a little better knowing that someone was getting it worse. The other horror story class turned out to be operative dentistry. There wasn't as much continual pressure since you didn't get marked every week but when it came time for our first practical exam the tension had reached vein-popping levels. Taking place in our seventh week the timing played a crucial part in the overall stress level since the next week we had our first set of written exams. The sheer volume of material we had to memorize was vast. We were all trying to cram histology anatomy, biochemistry, physiology, dental occlusion, dental material sciences and operative dentistry into our virginal brains, while trying to get lots of rest so we could perform with a steady hand for our practical exam. This tactic of mental and physical overload was one that was used repeatedly. The idea was to see how much garbage you could retain and then regurgitate under as stressful conditions as possible. And then on top of that be expected to perform unfailingly the most difficult and precise manual tasks. I didn't sleep well the night before our first practical exam in operative dentistry. I had a vivid dream of sitting in a lecture class with no clothes on.

The practical exam assignment we were given was so easy, it would take the average dentist about thirty seconds to do in real life. For first year dental students it was a formidable and intimidating challenge. We had to drill out the central groove region of a lower first molar to a uniform five millimeter depth. The instructors were looking for perfectly executed cuts, straight ninety degree angles and smoother than smooth floors and walls on our preparations. Dr Willis and his assistants watched us like hawks eagerly searching for students who appeared frazzled. That was another important aspect of dental school behavior that we all seemed to know instinctively, even at this early level. Never let them see you sweat. No matter how wrong things were going it was essential to at least look like you knew what you were doing, that you were in control. I may have looked in control but I was getting off to a lousy start.My nervousness was causing my hands to shake. On the first cut with the drill I went about two millimeters too deep in the central portion of the tooth. I'd either have to make the whole floor of the tooth prep two millimeters too deep or else tilt the floor and try to make the tilt as smooth as possible. Either way I was going to get penalized. Choosing the lesser of two evils I decided to make the whole floor too deep.

Unfortunately I didn't have a chance to finish in our allotted thirty minutes.

One of the most unpleasant aspects of the practical exam was that the exam was marked immediately and the marks were posted right after that. I was in the cafeteria working on the battery acid-like beverage they claimed was coffee when a classmate came in,all out of breath and announced that the marks had been posted.

I half ran, half walked down to the display case where the green sheet with our marks was displayed behind glass. For the purpose of privacy we had all been assigned our own secret four digit I.D. number and beside these numbers were our marks. It took me awhile to find my number and when I saw my mark I felt sick. Fifty-seven percent. Just to make sure,I double and even triple-checked my mark. Quickly I counted the other failures and came up with six others. Someone had even gotten a twenty percent.

Walking away from the case I felt devastated. I stumbled to the nearest washroom, sat down in a cubicle and cried. I couldn't believe it. How would I be able to study for my written exams feeling the way I was. Did I have what it would take to be a dentist?

Failure was not in my background. Before dental school the only test I'd ever failed was my eye exam in grade five, when I discovered I needed to wear eyeglasses.

But from adversity comes strength. Somewhere from the hidden recesses of my depressed brain

I remembered those words. I was realizing that dental school was going to be tough. I'd have to put my nose to the grindstone, grit my teeth and fight. I'd always have to try my best and there was no room for slacking off.

To counteract my setback in operative dentistry I studied twice as hard for my written exams. Yet despite my inspired efforts I still wasn't prepared for the written exams at the end of first quarter. All the exams were multiple choice. I hadn't written a multiple choice exam in over two years. To make matters worse, the multiple choice questions were not straight-forward like:

What is the chemical symbol for Carbon?
A. Cu
B. Cn
C. C
D. Car
Choose the correct answer.

Instead they were all like:

If you increase the respiratory rate in a hypoxic individual what happens?
1.heart rate increases
2.blood pressure increases
3.arterial oxygen increases
4.cardiac output increases
5.nausea
A. If 1 and 2 are correct
B. If 2 and 4 are correct
C. If 1,2 and 3 are correct
D. If all are correct
E. If none are correct

With these types of questions you had to know your material inside out. If you just memorized, chances were you wouldn't have enough room in your brain to memorize all you needed to know. For instance with the above example you might have memorized what happened to cardiac output, blood pressure, arterial oxygen and heart rate when respiratory rate increased but chances are you wouldn't have memorized these changes in a hypoxic individual.

Trying to figure out the answer to a question like this would take at least five to ten minutes, and in the end you might be guessing anyway. And then you'd still have forty-nine more questions and only fifty minutes left.

Altogether over four days we wrote six exams,-biochemistry, histology, physiology, gross anatomy, dental material sciences and operative dentistry. The most memorable was gross anatomy.

The exam was in two parts. A multiple choice written section and a bell-ringer lab section. The bell-ringer exam was gruesome. There were thirty different numbered stations. At each of these stations there was a dead body or a dead body part. Most of these were sliced open to expose the structure, muscle, nerve, vein, artery or bone in question indicated with a red pin. We had to identify the indicated structure and state its function. At precisely ninety second intervals Dr Boch would merrily ring a bell and we'd move on to the next ghastly scenario.

It was kind of like visiting thirty different car accidents or murder sites. I remember vividly that one of the structures we had to identify was a clitoris. I wondered how many in our class would get that one wrong

Like the female med student in our physiology class. She asked the lecturer if it was a requisite for the male to sleep after orgasm had been achieved.

When our six exams were finished I was exhausted. I'd studied harder than I'd ever studied before, yet I really had no idea how I'd done.

Our second dental pub was held the same day as our last exam. It was good timing. Dental pubs were the social highlight of our faculty. Every year there were four and they coincided with the end of our exams. They were always held at the Great Hall and they were always packed.

About a third of the people were dental students and their friends and the other two thirds were mostly girls looking to meet dental students. The majority of the girls came from other health sciences faculties like nursing or occupational health. Many were looking for their MRS degrees.

✳ ✳ ✳

There was a kind of unwritten, unspoken hierarchy at these pubs. If you were a   dental student you could get almost any girl to dance with you. But ,if she found out you were only in first year, chances were she would go looking for a higher year student. Fourth year had it the best, being the closest to graduation and making money. They were in the highest demand. Many girls didn't want to wait three or four years to get a rock and subsequent annual or biannual trips to the Carribean. It was a little sickening.

Ellen was in Toronto and things were already starting to cool off between us because of the long distance factor. The other factor was her insistence on staying a virgin. I tried not to make a big deal about it, but now that we had been exclusive for almost two months I thought it was time to make a move. She wanted to stay a virgin until she was at least engaged and I didn't see that in our near or distant future. She was way too social for me. All I wanted to do during my time off was lie around and sleep and all she wanted to do was hang out with her friends. So when I went to the pub that night I went with the idea of being single. I ended up meeting a gorgeous brunette in her third year of communicative disorders. She was a knockout and after a few cold beers, a few dances and lots of small talk I thought we were developing a rapport. I turned around to get another beer and she disappeared. When I saw her next she was cheek to cheek, slow dancing with a guy in fourth year. It was like I didn't exist anymore.

As the night went on I drank more and ended up having a great time bitching about our exams and dancing with some of the girls in our class. There was no feeling of passion or excitement during these dances but instead a warm feeling of just being together and having fun. I danced like a madman with flailing arms and legs to David Bowie's White Wedding. I noticed others looking at me oddly but I didn't care. I was dancing to forget, letting out my frustrations on the dance floor. When I got home later that night I lay in bed for a long time reflecting on the last eight weeks.- Time was going by fast, I had now done a quarter of first year. I couldn't sleep so I ended up phoning Ellen. In retrospect it was probably a bad idea because of my melancholy mood. "Hi, I hope I'm not phoning too late", I started. "It's two o'clock in the morning- are you nuts?" She answered.. "I've been thinking about you and us and I don't think it's going to work,

I think we're too different to make things work. You just want to spend time with your friends and I can't stand your friends," She countered, "-Look, Ken, I can't help it if you're depressed all the time. At least my friends make me laugh. Now, let me get this right, you want to break up right now, over the phone like this." She laughed. "Well-it doesn't seem to be working out does it?" I responded. When she laughed I felt about two inches tall. Suddenly I didn't want to break up with her. "You're right,Ken, it's not working out and you know what else, I don't think I even like you right now. You think you're so great because you're a dental student. That doesn't mean a thing to me. I don't see much of a future for us." I started to cry. "No, Ellen don't leave me, please give me another chance."She answered, "Are you starting to cry? You're the one who wanted to break up with me. What is the matter with you?"

We ended up saying goodnight but not goodbye, at least not yet.

At the end of first quarter we had student elections. We needed to elect a class president, to act as a liaison between students and faculty. The problem was that nobody wanted the position. We all sat around feeling uncomfortable, looking at the floor or ceiling Finally Tom Johnson put up his hand. He was the tall,surfer dude who'd been in my gross anatomy group. He said, "I'll be class president as long as no one tells me what to do, cuz I just don't give a shit." There were no objections. He ended up being our class president for the next four years. His attitude was, "I don't give a shit." That was also his personal mantra that he used to survive the horrors of dental school. And it worked well for our class president. After a while his nickname became " The Pres " He made an absolutely great class president because he truly didn't give a shit.

When our second quarter started there were a few changes in our schedule. Instead of gross anatomy we were now taking anatomy of the head and neck region. As part of the course we were each assigned a real human skull. Eventually we would be responsible for knowing every bone, muscle, attachment, bump and hole on the skulls. We also had to learn the paths of every major nerve, vein and artery. Before dental school had started this would have seemed quite macabre, but after the blood and guts of gross anatomy, the skull didn't faze me at all.

* * *

My roommates were fascinated with the skull and like little boys they loved to take it out of its case and play with it.

During the first week of the second quarter we learned the results of our exams. My highest mark was in biochemistry,(eighty-eight percent)and my lowest was in physiology (sixty-eight percent).I had seventy-three percent in gross anatomy, seventy-eight percent in histology, seventy-four percent in operative dentistry and eighty-one percent in D.M.S. Compared to the rest of the class my marks were still higher than average, but it wasn't much consolation. I was used to getting eighties and nineties. In fact my grade point average when I applied to dental school was eighty-five percent.

I found it strange that we were given actual numeric grades because on our final report card we only got one of three marks. H for honors, P for pass and F for fail. Sixty percent was the cut off between pass and fail and anything eighty percent or above was honors.

By the beginning of second quarter I was beginning to notice changes within myself. My personality was changing in a myriad of subtle ways and I wasn't positive I was liking the changes. First of all, I was becoming more anti-social. Being surrounded by people all day in class and then my roommates all night was starting to get to me. I needed space and time to myself. Not having that privacy was making me miserable.

The constant pressure to read and study was also getting to me. There seemed to be only so much time to learn and not near enough time to learn it all. I think my parents noticed my growing frustration when I went home for Thanksgiving. I had mentioned that dental school was not what I thought it would be and I was met by blank stares from my parents,

My parents were very pragmatic people and they knew probably even better than I, how difficult the next four years would be-They reassured me as best as they could, Everything worth-while took a lot of work and sweat, and furthermore if dental school was easy, then anyone could be a dentist. My mom told me how proud she was of me already just for getting accepted to dental school. My dad was less forthcoming. In fact when he found out I was accepted he never said a word to me about it. Instead he left me a teletype message on my study table at home. He worked as a night editor at the local paper and he had removed the teletype article from the machine. The article stated how in ten years from now there was going to be a glut of dentists in Ontario.

I couldn't believe it. Not only couldn't he acknowledge my acceptance, he had to piss on it too.

When I got back to school on the train holiday Monday I felt just as lousy as I had before the weekend. I hadn't seen Ellen in two weekends and I had to admit to myself it was over. She never phoned me anymore, I had to do all the calling and most of the time she couldn't wait to get off the phone with me. I added insult to injury by not seeing her on the long weekend. When I called her on holiday Monday I just left her a message. " It's over, do me a favor don't call me." And that was that. I never heard from her again.

Slowly, very slowly, first year went by. Our second set of exams just before the Christmas break seemed even worse than our first. Probably because we'd taken a significantly greater amount of lecture and reading material. It should be reassuring to the average dental patient to know their dentist was taught the names of all twelve cranial nerves or fifteen branches of the facial artery. It was often difficult to filter out what was important and what was not.

I made a point to study especially hard for the Christmas physiology exam because I wanted to prove to myself I was as smart or smarter than the average med student. On the first physiology exam the dental students' average was ten percent lower than for the med students. So I studied as hard as I could for the second physiology exam. I was practically breathing physiology. I ended up with eighty-seven percent on the second exam. My mark was twelve percent higher than the average med student and twenty-five percent higher than the average dental student. It was a rare moment of personal triumph for me.

Unfortunately my victory in physiology was isolated. My other marks for the Christmas exams ranged from sixty-five to seventy-five percent. Overall it was pretty mediocre.

A long-standing tradition at the dental school was Skit Night. It was always held just before Christmas vacation. We sang songs and made up skits to poke fun at the dental school staff. It was our chance to exact revenge on them. As a first year class we didn't really know what was expected, so we didn't take any chances. We kept things pretty respectable. Unlike the skits from the senior classes, especially the fourth year class.

I was in one of our skits. We did a spoof on the Police song, "Every breath you take."

I wore one of our white dental smocks with black electrical tape wrapped around the smock in horizontal bands. I looked like a jailbird. There were three of us that posed as students and we had two students from our class who acted as instructors. We took liberty with the words of the song. Our version went like this. "Every breath you take, Every prep you make, Every tooth you break, Every step you take, I'll be watching you." The refrain was. "0 can't you see, you belong to me, How my poor heart breaks with every U you make." Our other skits were just as tame.

I couldn't believe what the fourth year students did. First of all they dressed up as the profs in cruel parodies. In real life Dr Boch wore a toupee. They took the head of a mop, died it black and plopped it over the head of the student who was portraying Dr Bock. For Dr Moore they used a three-foot doll, with someone behind it speaking his lines. Dr Moore was quite short but I think they crossed the line with the doll. There were a lot of other profs who we didn't know yet who were similarly portrayed. They did a skit that was a parody of the Dating Game. There was a beautiful young woman who asked questions of three profs who were not visible to her. The three profs were Dr Boch, Dr Moore, and an obviously oriental prof with a big pot belly. The girl started her questions."Bachelor number one,- If we were on a first date where would you take me?" Dr Boch was bachelor number one. He said, "I would take you to my house, I'd introduce you to my mom, and then I would take you to my room, in the basement"-"Bachelor number two,-same question," the pretty girl asked. The unknown oriental was bachelor number two. He spoke with an affected Chineses accent. "I take you in the bum." "Oh bachelor number two, that was very naughty," the girl purred. "Bachelor number three,what do you like to do for fun?"she asked. Bachelor number three was Dr Moore, "Well I like to masturbate and I like traveling, I've been to Corn Hole Alabama, and hnstillavirgin, Ireland." " Very nice, bachelor number three,my next question is for bachelor number two, If we were to get married what would we do on our wedding night?" Bachelor number two replied, "First we would take bath together in ice water, then you would lie on bed very still, not to move- not to talk, then we make whooppee." "Oh bachelor number two, that sounds a little creepy. Bachelor number one, same question please," she asked.Bachelor number one replied, "Well I would buy a Polaroid camera and ten rolls of film, and take pictures of you with no clothes-.Then we would make whooppee as long as you promise not to laugh at how small my weenie is." "Oh bachelor number one, that doesn't sound so good. Bachelor number three, same question," she queried. Bachelor number three said, "If you can find my weenie we will make whoopee. If you can't find it we can play Barry Manilow songs on the stereo, while I make egg salad sandwiches and tang." The game show host interrupted. "Well our lovely bachelorette has a lot to think over. We'll give her a little time to make her decision." After about a five second pause, he continued, "Bachelorette, which of our under-endowed bachelors would you like to choose?" She said, "Well it's a tough choice, but I'll go with bachelor number two." The oriental prof came around from behind the barrier and made a bee line right for the girl.He hugged her to his body and lifted her into the air. The bachelorette screamed, "OH SHIT!! " The curtain came down and the skit was over. The whole evening was hilarious and by the time it was over my stomach hurt from laughing so hard.

To celebrate the last of our exams before Christmas I went out to get plastered with a couple of my roommates and Dan. We finished our last exam at five o'clock and from there Dan and I went to my house. Snow was coming down with a vengeance and with the howling winds and sub-normal temperatures that evening was developing into a full-blown blizzard.

After four or five beers at the house we decided to brave the elements and hopped on a bus going downtown. Our destination, Ichabod's, a slimy, greasy, disco-type bar was practically deserted. Eventually by nine o'clock it started to fill up. I spent most of the evening chatting up a cashier from Woolco. She was gorgeous and seemed interested in getting to know me better. Eventually because I got so drunk I lost track of her. Just before closing I stole a stuffed duck. It was a genuine taxidermist grade mallard that was hanging on the wall beside the dance floor.I just reached up, yanked it off the wall and stuffed it into my jacket.

We missed the last bus and couldn't find a cab, so we ended up walking home in the blizzard. Halfway home I fought Dan for the duck and I ended up biting its head off.

When we finally made it back we were exhausted, half frozen and very drunk. The first object I saw when I opened the door to my room was the skull.

Without even thinking I grabbed the skull and threw it as hard as I could against the far wall of my bedroom. Like stealing the duck, I don't know why I did it. Frustration? Bitterness?

* * *

Anger? Maybe the skull was a symbol of all I despised and hated about dental school. The skull shattered into hundreds of pieces but at the time I didn't care. I was drunk as a skunk

In the morning I gazed with horror at the pieces of skull scattered across the floor. Ironically my rash and stupid move the night before forced me to learn my anatomy. like a three dimensional jigsaw puzzle I glued the whole skull back together again with crazy glue. It took me months but by the time I had finished I knew every square millimeter, every bump, indentation and groove.

The Christmas holiday flew by in a flash. It was wonderful having two and a half weeks to do nothing. I managed to get together with a couple friends from high school that I hadn't seen since before I was accepted into dental school. We talked about old times mostly, but the conversation felt artificial and strained. They kept on joking about the BMW I'd soon be driving and on the surface it was all quite amusing. In reality they were resentful and after several more beers it became obvious. It was hard to take . I wasn't used to being made to feel guilty for choosing to better myself. I just wanted to get away. They suggested going to a hamburger joint for a late night snack and I declined, feigning tiredness. It would be that way with many of my past friends. As the years of dental school went by I would lose touch with most of my previous friends.

I thought it would be different when I went out with my two best friends from Chemistry, Rob and Tom. We'd shared a lot during our last four years in Chemistry. But while they only had one more year of studies, I still had four years ahead of me. When we got together I felt a certain chill in the air.

We'd had a few drinks when Torn started, "You know it feels like you're bailing out on us, buddy." I replied, " I honestly didn't think I'd get accepted. This is as much a surprise to me as it is to you guys. I'll still come down on weekends and hang out with you. " Rob said, " Yeah right, you and your new Rolex." "Guys, give me a break, I'm still a poor student, at least for the next four years. I'm the same guy. I haven't changed just because I'm now studying dentistry instead of chemistry," I replied. Rob countered, "Yeah, you say that now but when you're a big hot shot dentist you won't want to hang out with us any more." "C'mon guys, gimme a break will ya? Why would I want to hang around with a bunch of losers like you anyways?" I said. Instead of coming across as a joke, my last comment just sat there,like dead air. I think I was a little resentful of them as well.They could sail through their last year of school while I was working my ass off just to pass.

I tried going back in the new year with a more positive attitude. I was hoping things would get better. In reality things got worse. The only real improvement in the new year was due to a new instructor in my dental occlusion course. Dr Penn was in her early thirties and where Dr Rabst had been cruel and sadistic, Dr Penn was caring and kind. The tension headaches on Tuesday afternoons started disappearing. I was actually beginning to enjoy our wax-up exercises. Instead of building up individual teeth we were now waxing up an entire half arch of eight teeth from a central incisor to a second molar. The emphasis was now on occlusion or how the teeth came together.

On these eight teeth we had to make them come together and touch the opposing eight teeth in fifty two exact spots. Initially this sounded impossible, but as time went by- under Dr Perm's patient tutelage, the wax started shaping up and clicking into place. It was important that we stay within the curve of Spee. The curve of Spee was an imaginary line that went from the incisal edge of the central maxillary incisor to the incisal edges of all the posterior teeth. We used to joke about going beyond the curve of Spee, of walking out of dental school and never coming back.

In our academic courses it seemed like we were getting more and more reading assignments. By the end of January I was hundreds of pages behind in my reading.

At the house I was in the middle of a cold war with me against them. Tim's late night TV and almost constant partying prompted me to drastic measures. Night after night I'd storm out of my bedroom to turn the volume of the TV down. In the morning at seven thirty I'd bang around as loudly as I could and sing at the top of my lungs in the shower.

Tim's earliest course all year started at noon but I knew he was a light sleeper so my antics were at least somewhat effective.

We fought over who drank whose milk or whose day it was to do the dishes. By so called democratic vote I ended up washing stacks and stacks of crusted-over plates and dishes far more often than was democratic. After a while I started avoiding the house as much as possible and basically only went there to sleep. I started eating dinner at school and studying in one of the many libraries until nine or ten at night. I'd become the pariah of the house.

During the weekend things were different. By unspoken agreement the cold war ended with the end of the school week.. I ended up going to a lot of bars and parties with them. I think by bringing me along, a dental student, they felt their prestige was elevated. It would have been better if I had been a medical student, but unfortunately I was all they could get. We'd be at a party for a half hour or so when I'd hear some co-ed whisper to another, "So which one is in dentistry?" Generally, dental students were good catches for a MRS degree-definitely better than normal undergraduate students.

I was at a party with three of my roommates in February when I met Shelley. I was attracted to her from the moment I first laid eyes on her. She had dark, shoulder length hair, a strikingly beautiful face and a pleasantly rounded figure. I stared at her from across the crowded room and as if on cue she looked right at me and smiled. I felt a tingling at the back of my neck. I went over right away and introduced myself. We clicked. She was studying nursing just like Ellen had been and in fact they even knew each other. We talked for hours and by the end of the evening I had her phone number. Although we lived almost two hundred miles apart we started a relationship. She was the best looking girl I'd ever gone out with. We had the commonality of being in school and at times we were even learning the same or complimentary material at the same time. While she poked and prodded my liver and spleen I tried to find ways to get to her more private parts. At least she wasn't a virgin.

Shelley helped me make it through the rest of first year. We saw each other practically every weekend and when we were together I forgot about how awful dental school was. She was one of those people who was always happy. She had a zest for life and a way of looking at the world around her which made even the most mundane tasks seem fun.

Our third set of exams came and went. Before our final eight weeks we had a week off. I spent four days with Shelley. Conveniently her parents were in Florida for the week so we had her parents' place to ourselves. The weather was cold and bleak but we didn't care. We were in love.

Others in my class took the week off to go south and came back almost black from the sun. I was jealous because I couldn't afford the luxury. Ironically one of the girls who went to the Bahamas had also received a grant from the faculty for being financially in need. Every year she would go away at Christmas and the March break and every year she was the sole recipient of the "Student in need" grant. It was such a joke. Everyone except the faculty knew her parents were loaded.

It was in the last quarter of first year that we had the chance to go to the main clinic. We each picked a partner from the class and took turns looking in each other's mouths and then eventually cleaning each other's teeth.

It felt strange putting our mouth mirrors and dental explorers actually into a real person's mouth. Compared to the plastic dentoform teeth we'd been working on it was amazing how different real teeth looked. To complicate matters the tongue and cheeks were always getting in the way and saliva was everywhere.

The last part of the year seemed to speed up and before we knew it we were studying for final exams. We had eleven exams all together, about one a day for two weeks.

I found it impossible to study at home. My roommates had finished their classes and each had about four or five exams in roughly a three-week time span. Which meant Party.Party,Party to them anyway. The weather didn't help. It was an early summer with clear azure blue skies and escalating temperatures.

* * *

I did most of my studying at the University. I went to the twelfth floor of the Social Sciences
building and sat in an armchair looking out over the whole city. Nobody else was around at night so it made an ideal study spot.

By the time I made it home after midnight I'd go straight to sleep. Our classes ended on a Friday and our first exam was on the next Monday. Studying was strictly memorization. You didn't have to be smart. All you needed was a good memory.

Somehow the eleven exams and two weeks passed.

My report card came in early June. Hesitantly I opened the envelope. My hands betrayed me by shaking like a leaf as I read the letter. I'd passed all my courses and even ended up with two honors,one in biochemistry and one in oral histology. The main thing was that I didn't have to come back in the summer to write any supplemental exams. I had successfully finished first year.

I found out later that twelve students had failed one or more courses in first year and had to go back to write make-up or supplemental exams. I wasn't surprised to learn that Marcus had to do two practical and two written supplemental exams.

For the summer I worked in the quality control lab at a local brewery. We tested for color, Ph, pCO2 and alcohol content. On weekends Shelley and I spent time together and dental school seemed far away and distant.

By the end of first year I knew I wouldn't be able to survive another year living in the house.

I'd applied to the on-campus one-bedroom apartments. I was accepted in May and had moved all my possessions to my new apartment in early June. It was a mere five minutes' stroll from the Dental Sciences building. I could sleep in an extra twenty or thirty minutes every morning. The downside to living so close was that I never felt like I got away from dental school. All I had to do was look out my bedroom window and I could see the Dental Sciences building looming threateningly in the foreground. After a while I felt the presence of school, even in my sleep and dreams.

The walls in the new apartment were paper-thin and you could tell when the person upstairs used their washroom. You could even tell if they'd gone number one or number two. But at least there was no Late Night with David Letterman. And for that I was grateful.

A week before second year started I went into a full-blown depression. I spent the last weekend of the summer doing absolutely nothing. I was miserable the whole time. The thought of going back for another year loomed hideously before me. I knew second year would be less academic and more "hands on". Ironically I found from first year that the courses I had enjoyed more had been the academic ones. The ones I hated the most had been the "hands on" courses. Despite passing first year my confidence was still at a fairly low level. I even thought briefly of quitting but it wasn't a serious consideration because I had no alternate plans for the future. I was committed to another year of dental school.

When I was accepted to the one-bedroom apartments on campus, I told my roommate Tim that I would be moving out of the house at the end of May. And since I was no longer at the house I wouldn't be paying rent anymore. Tim told me in no uncertain terms that I had to pay rent until September. He threatened that he would lock up my stereo and other valuables if I didn't pay. I was pissed. But I really didn't have much choice.

So I thought of what I could do to get him back. I put an ad in the paper for a sublet from June until September. I knew I had the right sublet when I spoke to him on the phone. He told me that he'd just got out of prison and really needed a place for himself and his pregnant girlfriend to stay for the summer. My discount rate of two hundred and fifty dollars a month definitely sweetened the deal. I was still losing a hundred and fifty dollars a month, but that didn't really matter to me.

I was happy that I could leave my roommates with a parting gift. That was the least I could do after being their whipping boy for the whole year. I have to admit that I was amused by their antics. One morning I woke up to find a wheelchair at the bottom of the stairs. Tim had picked up a girl at the pub. It didn't seem to bother him that she couldn't walk. He brought her home and simply carried her up to his bedroom. It was a little awkward in the morning. It seemed Tim's new girlfriend didn't want to leave. He finally had to carry her kicking and screaming down the stairs. He had to forcibly push her wheelchair out the door. Tim told us later that she shit and pissed all over his bed sheets. He had to carry her into the bathroom and get her all cleaned up before she could go. We teased Tim relentlessly over his little escapade.

The only thing my roommates wanted was to get laid. And they would do anything for it. Tim told one girl he was a third year med student, but blew it when she asked him where his uvula was. He said only women had uvulas. She laughed and said, " Nice try ,"

During the summer I spent too much time with my parents. I think they felt like they were losing me, because they kept telling me the stories of my roots, again and again. As if they could still mold me by the manifest destiny of my genes.

My father's father, Mika, was the son of a wealthy landowner in Finland. Mika married at a young age and soon there after had a son. When he got the maid pregnant, rather then face his wife and family, he took off with the pregnant maid to Canada. Upon arrival in Canada he changed his name from Tikkonen to Spaldane, and he stayed with the maid. The maid's child was my father. Officially my father was a bastard. Mika was a womanizer and a heavy drinker, who had no interest in raising my dad. There were no father and son picnics. My father's mother over-compensated for the lack of paternal care, by spoiling my dad rotten. He had all his teeth extracted when he was sixteen, because he was given so many sweets from his mom. For his seventeenth birthday, he was awarded with a brand new set of dentures that he wore for the next thirty years, until they eventually broke down. I was hoping that when I graduated from dental school that my dad would ask me to make him a brand new set of dentures.

My mother's mother, Paulina, was a Pole who came to Canada on a ship, in between world war one and world war two. She was transported by train to be settled in the prairies. When she heard that the prairies were truly a dismal place, she simply hopped off the train in Thunder Bay. All she had were the clothes on her back and a few dollars in her pockets. She had a job in two days and was renting an apartment within a week.

It took her a little longer to find a husband. Anthony was seventeen years older than her and he'd arrived in Canada right after world war one-, from the Ukraine. He had a good job with CN

Rail and by the time he met Paulina, he already owned his own house. Because of their age difference Anthony thought he had little chance of capturing such a beautiful and headstrong woman. Finally he came up with an idea. He approached the lovely Paulina with a request. He said that he had saved two thousand dollars and he didn't know what do with it. He didn't trust the banks and he wondered if she could possibly hold the money for him. She said "My pleasure." One thing led to another and eventually they married. Anthony never did get his money back.

My parents met in bed. They were both at a party one fine summer night in Thunder Bay. My mother had been working all day as a counselor at a children's camp. By the time she got to the party she was exhausted, so she snuck into one of the bedrooms and lay down to rest. She remembers hearing one man's very irritating, very loud monotone voice that seemed to rise above the general din of the party. She must have fallen asleep for a while, because next thing she knew someone had plopped down on the bed beside her. It was my father. They started talking and kept talking until the end of the party. By the end of the night my dad was brushing my mom's hair.She thought his voice sounded familiar, and finally realized that my father was the man with the very irritating voice. My dad was mesmerized by this remarkably intelligent women with the lustrous, long hair. He was hooked and it was only a matter of time before they wed. Their set of values and morals were identical. Neither of them believed in God. Instead they were convinced of man's humanitarianism. Despite evidence to the contrary, they believed in the goodness of their fellow man. Socialism was their anthem and we, their children-, were their guinea pigs in the great experiment. Despite or maybe because they were non-materialistic people, they had managed to save at least a million dollars by the time I entered dentistry. I don't think they had any idea what to do with their money. They still had the original appliances in their house from when they had married thirty years earlier. I was going to have to map my own place in the world because I simply could not imagine a life without God. I was going to be the only believer in a family of Pagans.

Second Year

We started second year with one fewer student. Anna, an older, divorced former Romanian dentist had failed one of her supplemental exams. Subsequently she was asked to leave the faculty of dentistry. Anna had been somewhat mysterious to the rest of the class. She had looked and dressed like a high-priced hooker with her beached blonde hair, fish-net stockings, high stilettos and slutty push-up dresses. It was rumored she'd been having an affair with Dr Willis of the operative dentistry department. After she was asked to leave, Anna sued the faculty of dentistry for wrongful dismissal. Remarkably she won her case but instead of coming back for the second year she settled for cash and opened up an Aesthetique Nail Clinic instead.

The schedule for second year was identical to first year. Eight thirty to five o'clock, five days a week. Most of what we'd be doing in second year was in preparation for the clinic. All the manual skills we'd soon need to work on real live patients were learned, practiced and perfected in our second year lab. The lab would become a home away from home since we'd end up spending so much of our time there. My assigned seat in the lab was between Dan and Marcus. I was only two seats from the front of B Row, Seat B2.

Instead of eleven different courses we now had twenty-one. Dental material sciences, dental occlusion, endodontics, fixed prosthodontics, fixed prosthodontics lab, microbiology, operative dentistry, operative dentistry lab, oral medicine, oral microbiology, oral microbiology lab, oral pathology, oral radiology, oral surgery, orthodontics, pathology, pharmacology, pediatric dentistry,periodontics, removable prosthodontics and removable prosthodontics lab.(-Whew!-) I think the worst was knowing we'd eventually have twenty-one final exams.

Since I sat beside Marcus I made a point to get to know him. He came from a solid middle class family, that, like mine, stressed education. He was an only child and his mom still doted on him. When he went home for the weekends he came back with all his meals,wrapped in tin foil and frozen. All he had to do was take it out of the freezer and heat it up. They were even dated from Monday to Sunday so he knew which meal to eat on which day.

When you talked to Marcus you got a funny feeling that his elevator didn't go to the top floor. It wasn't in your face obvious. It was much more subtle. When we first started second year I asked, " So Marcus, how was your summer?" He responded," Oh it was great, just great, I had a great summer." " But didn't you have to do some supplemental exams? ", I prodded. "Oh yeah, that. Yeah they went great, no problem at all,"he said. "Yeah, but weren't you scared ? I mean if you failed one, you would have gotten kicked out, wouldn't you?" I queried. "Oh no, they all went well. Besides, my mom said that if they kicked me out I could sue them." "How could you sue them? I mean on what grounds could you sue them? " I wanted to know. "My mom said it was no problem, it would be easy, besides I'm here aren't I ?" His logic made sense in a weird kind of way.

"So-, Marcus, did you get laid this summer?" I asked. Marcus was tall, dark and handsome, except for a too large nose. In response to my question he looked awkward and constipated and he said, "I don't have a girlfriend, I've never had a girlfriend yet." I had to ask, "You mean you've never had a girlfriend, ever." "No, I've never had time, I've always been too busy with school," he replied. Marcus was a virgin. And in a strange kind of way he was actually clueless about dating, about women, about sex, about a lot of things. From the exterior he looked like a handsome GQ kind of guy, but on the inside he was still a child. I think it was his child like vulnerability that made him such a target for the dental instructors. He had absolutely "no balls." If you insulted him, he thanked you, and if you argued with him, he instantly agreed with you. His dental school experience was going to be a true nightmare unless he got tougher.

I tried to help him, I couldn't stand the way the instructors bullied him and the way most of my classmates treated him with open contempt. "Come on Marcus, don't get discouraged, you're going to be one of the best dentists out there, with your super kind heart. Most of the assholes in our class will be ripping off their patients left, right and center. But you're going to be the most ethical guy that has ever graduated from this faculty." I tried building him up as much as I could. But it seemed to no avail. Eventually I got tired as he sunk lower and lower, as his marks submerged to subterranean levels. I had to keep my ship afloat and I had no time to be a rescuer. Dan, who was on the other side of me was almost a polar opposite of Marcus. In second year Dan joined the army. He simply ran out of money to be able to continue his education by any other way. The army paid you an annual stipend as well as paying all your dental school costs. The only catch was that you had to serve in the Armed Forces for a total of four years, or three years as in Dan's case. Dan didn't really fit in with the other guys in our class that were in the Army, Dan was just a little too warped for them.

When we first got back from the summer I asked Dan, "So how was your time off, big guy?" "To be honest it sucked. I had to do basic training. And nobody in the Army has a sense of fucking humor. I outran,outshot,outmarched,outtrained, outexercised and outdrank all those pansy asses, and they didn't even give me a medal." I laughed. "So how do you think second year's going to be, hot shot?" He replied, "Well just between you and me I think this is the year that Marcus is going to get sent home. And the exams are going to be a bitch." I agreed. Looking on the positive side second year couldn't be all that bad since we still didn't have patients. We could go out any night of the week, have as many drinks as we wanted and it didn't matter because the next day we'd just be sitting in a classroom or at the very worst massacring the plastic teeth on a skinhead mannequin. In fact it became a tradition for a group of us to go out drinking

Thursday nights. Friday mornings we had our fixed prosthodontics course. An hour lecture and three hour lab. Being hung-over for fixed prosthodontics became routine for us.

Our loosely-knit social group consisted of myself, Paul, Dave Wong and Vijay. We all knew each other a little from first year but it wasn't until second year that we really started hanging out together.

Paul was about five feet,six inches tall with a slightly stalky build.Thick brownish hair parted in the center and cut fairly short gave Paul a boyish look. He had a flair for conversation and possessed a dynamic energy that often propelled him into trouble. Paul's unquenchable zest for life kept him going when the going got rough. And it often did because Paul was a guy whom the instructors loved to hate. With the exception of Marcus I don't think anyone else had such a hard time with the instructors.

Dave W would eventually become my best friend, He was funny, introspective and smart. He had no time for bullshit and he despised most of our instructors. If you needed help he was always there. He had a unique way of looking at the world and he always made me laugh.

If an award was presented to the most laid-back person in our class, Vijay would win, hands down. I never once saw him upset or angry at anything or anyone. To me, Vijay looked like Omar Shariff. With his coffee-colored skin he was often labeled as a Paki, which was incorrect since Vijay was born and raised in Canada. His dad and mom were both senior scientists with the Federal government and they both came from the same village in India. Vijay was the quietest of us all. He also had the best hands in the class. I think he was gifted. When I saw the wax-ups he had carved I was always in awe. His work looked so perfect you'd swear you were looking at a natural tooth and not a carving. Yet Vijay's talent never went to his head. He never became an arrogant prima donna like so many others in our class who only thought they were good.

Besides our four-some,-there were other groups. There were the glamour girls, the army guys and the out-to-lunch bunch as well as other groups, groupings and twosomes.The out-to-lunch bunch consisted of six guys who thought they were God's gift to dentistry and women. The profs loved them because they were such consummate ass-kissers. Everyone else despised them.

The glamour girls were the four best-looking girls in the class. They all wore designer labels and knew nothing about dentistry. Most of their work was completed by male instructors. If they ran into problems all they had to do was bat an eyelash or shed a tear until help arrived.

The army guys were the four who'd joined the Canadian Army to pay their way through school. They all had buzz-cuts and looked vaguely alike. In general they were a good bunch. Although the groups usually stuck together there was quite a bit of lateral movement between individual members of the various groups. For instance, members of the army group would sometimes hang out with the elite members of the out-to-lunch bunch. On the other hand some groups totally avoided the members of other groups. A prime example was the out-to-lunch bunch. They ignored everyone except the glamour girls and a few members of the army guys.

In second year we learned the nitty gritty technical aspects of dentistry. After learning the theory we tried it out on the fake dentoform teeth. We still weren't allowed near anything living with our drills.

In removable dentistry we each made a set of dentures, right from the initial impressions to the final completed denture. This task took six hours a week for sixteen weeks. It was from this assignment that most of us learned about frustration. Our lecturer and course director was Dr Keller. He had a mild-mannered voice, balding grey hair and an overall stoop-shouldered appearance. His nickname was ten after six, because he was always leaning to the right by about ten degrees. It looked like he'd been kicked around a little. For the most part Dr Keller was fair, but if you ended up on his shit list you were in trouble. The quickest way to end up on his shit list was to fail one or more of his surprise quizzes he loved to spring on the unsuspecting class. I was lucky because every time Dr Keller made the announcement to close our books I usually opened mine long enough to cram the necessary information in before his quizzes began. In this way I passed all his quizzes and ended up on the right side of his shit list.

Not so for my friend Paul who had the misfortune to fail every single quiz. This earned Paul several privileges. First he had the pleasure of attending a personal interview with Dr Keller to discus attitude and performance and second he ended up having to write the supplemental exam for second year removable prosthodontics. What was even worse was that Dr Keller would be breathing up Paul's ass in the clinic for the next two and a half years.

The frustration in removable started with our first lab session. All we had to do was take an impression of an artificial edentulous (no teeth) arch. It took most of us over ten hours and almost a hundred impressions. I remember on my first attempt ending up with an excellent impression. I couldn't believe it. There were no bubbles and I had captured the entire edentulous ridge in perfect detail. I brought it to Dr Keller for approval and maybe even a little praise. He took a cursory glance and asked how many impressions I'd taken. Proudly I announced it was my first try.

He looked at me skeptically, dug the point of his index finger into the impression material and said," Oops, sorry, you better try again." I couldn't believe it. I'd taken a great first impression and he deliberately wrecked it. Of course it took another thirty or forty more tries before I ended up with another good one. For each impression it took two minutes to mix, five minutes to set and then about another five minutes to clean up.

Our class went through so much impression material that we had to borrow extra garbage bags from the first year lab.

Once you had a good impression the next step was to pour it up in dental stone. This was another step where things usually went wrong. The first good impression I poured up ended up having huge air bubbles. This meant I bad to go back and start all over by taking a new impression. At least I wasn't alone. Most of the class was going through the same cycle of impressing and pouring up, over and over again. As an exercise it showed us all the different things that could go wrong in making a denture. Although discouraging, it was beneficial because it gave us a broad knowledge in denture fabrication, from the very first steps all the way to completion. By December we had all made a set of dentures.

I brought them home over the Christmas holidays and let the cat play with them. I dragged them around the kitchen floor on the end of a string. The cat went crazy pouncing, leaping and biting. It was the only biting that set of dentures ever had.

Another course with a lot of lab work was fixed prosthodontics. The course was split between its two co-directors, Dr Thomsky and Dr Moore. There couldn't have been a greater contrast between two people. Physically Dr Moore was short, petite, clean-shaven and fastidiously tidy in appearance. He always wore the lamest looking bowties.

Dr Thomsky was tall and looked a lot like Trapper John MD with his full beard, bald top, heavy build and slightly tired clothing. While Dr Moore lectured like a drill sergeant Dr Thomsky was much more casual with frequent jokes, sexual innuendos and a general care-free attitude.

Dr Moore and Dr Thomsky shared no love for each other. While one lectured the other would sit back and heckle. During our very first lecture Dr Moore was only a few minutes into his introductory remarks when Dr T. interrupted, "Uh excuse me Allan, you are incorrect with your date for the midterm." He pronounced Allan with the emphasis on the first syllable.

Dr T continued, "If you look closely on your schedule you can see quite clearly that the midterm is on October the twentieth, not October the twenty-first." Dr M stared out at Dr T with obvious distaste and coolly replied, "Yes the schedule may say October the twentieth, but if you will recall from our faculty advisory meeting in August, the date was changed to October the twenty-first." He paused and then added with obvious sarcasm, "You were at that meeting, weren't you, Fred?" Without missing a beat Dr T replied,"Yes you know I was there,Allan, and I don't remember that we changed the midterm date. I would advise you in the future to have your facts straight before you lecture." Since Dr T was a full professor and Dr M only an associate professor, Dr T was Dr M's superior. Because of this, Dr T usually won the arguments. Naturally these disagreements served as great entertainment value to our class.

Dr M was almost universally disliked from first year and it was satisfying to see him getting repeatedly humiliated.

Dr T soon became one of our most popular professors. He loved jokes and started every lecture with one. He was so approachable that I even went up to him after his second lecture and told him one of my favorite jokes.

He was at the front of the class after the lecture, surrounded by the usual sycophants and ass kissers. I moved my way right up there and asked him a minor question about the lecture material. He seemed a little annoyed and after his fairly abrupt response I asked him, "So what's yellow and lives off dead beatles?" He looked slightly amused and before he could think of a response I delivered the punch line, "Yoko Ono." His face cracked open into an ear-to-ear smile and he laughed out loud for almost a half minute. Still chuckling he asked, "What did you say your name was?" "Ken Spaldane,"I said. "Great joke, Ken," he added.

I guess I hit the right frequency with the Beatles joke because he always went out of his way to say hi to me after that.

Fixed prosthodontics was another course which had practical exams. I was all wound up for the first practical exam in fixed prosthodontics in early October. The odd thing was that the practical exam wasn't stressful. It seemed to be more like a friendly challenge. We all just tried our best. I ended up with an eighty-one percent on the first fixed practical exam.

There was no comparison between practical exams in fixed and operative dentistry. The tension during operative practical exams had been bad enough in first year. For second year the tension just seemed to get worse. The operative profs had the attitude that not everyone in dental school should be a dentist and they wanted to weed the rejects out. The atmosphere was predatory. They'd already gotten rid of Anna and almost gotten Marcus. They wanted new blood.

Fixed prosthodontics needed a higher degree of manual dexterity and skill than in operative dentistry, yet I barely scraped by
the practical operative exams in second year, while consistently
getting eighties for the fixed practical exams. It was obvious that
I didn't do well in a threatening atmosphere. In my personal life
my relationship with Shelley had steadily been sliding downhill
since the beginning of second year. She couldn't understand why
I was depressed all the time. I used to think we had a lot in common but more and more I could see we had divergent personali-
ties. Her idea of a fun evening was to get together with three or
four other couples and hang around like on Thirty-something.
I'd rather spend a private intimate evening alone with just her.

Finally one weekend in early November things came to a
head. I took the train on Friday evening to visit her. When I
arrived after my three-hour ride I was surprised she wasn't there
to meet me. I phoned her from the station and after five or six
rings she answered sounding as if she just woke up. "Oh hi, I
forgot you were coming today." She sounded distant and distracted and after a pause she continued, "Wait there, I'll come
and pick you up."

An hour later I was sitting in her car. She was wearing a
short green miniskirt and I couldn't keep my eyes off her creamy
white legs. "Uh," her hand was nervously tapping out a rhythm
on the steering wheel. "We're going to a party tonight, I hope
you don't mind. "

The party was a disaster.

So was the rest of the weekend.

By the time I was ready to take the train back, we both agreed
that it was over. And so when I got back I was miserable. School
sucked as badly as ever and my personal life was a shambles.
I desperately needed some female companionship. Of course I
wasn't the only one going through a rough time. The constant
criticism and almost all negative feedback was taking its toll.

In early December I had a bit of a fling with one of the girls in
our class. Barb was too individualistic to be in any one particular
group but she got along with almost everyone. We seemed to
be going through the same crisis. Dental school was making us

miserable and antisocial yet we both knew we were inherently happy and sociable people. Our fling started innocently enough with long discussions in the med-sci cafeteria and on the phone at night. Eventually we decided to get together on a Friday night to get drunk.

That Friday night we went through our individual life stories and three bottles of wine. It was no surprise that we ended up in bed. Unfortunately I only remember undressing and then waking up with a horrible hangover. All the rest was lost in an alcohol-induced blackout. That morning I felt like a skid. Everything had happened too fast. I knew I was still in love with Shelley. That night was the first and last for Barb and I. A week later she started going out with someone else. I was actually happy for her. Besides, there had been no real spark or passion between us. We were merely two lonely people who had very temporarily found solace in each other's arms.

Besides learning the nitty gritty technical aspects of dentistry we also took several courses that were actually interesting. Pharmacology, microbiology and pathology were my favorites.

I think I enjoyed these courses simply because they had nothing to do with teeth. Pharmacology was sort of an applied physiology. In fact if you knew your physiology you could actually determine how a certain drug would affect you, once you knew the drug's mechanism of action.

More practically we learned how to write a prescription and even what drugs we'd most commonly be prescribing. It amazed me that dentists were allowed to prescribe any prescription drug or medicine. It didn't seem to make sense since in reality dentists would only really need to prescribe a relatively small range of medications. With my previous background in biochemistry and chemistry, pharmacology just seemed to click.

Microbiology and pathology similarly fascinated me. Pathology is the study of disease along with the structural and functional manifestations. We first learned about diseases affecting the whole body and then we went into more detail with diseases of the oral cavity. We had two lecturers in pathology. Although they both had radically different styles they still managed to intersperse their rather morbid subject matter with dry humor and razor sharp wit. I imagine if you looked at slides of tumors all day long, day after day, eventually you'd become a little warped.

Microbiology is the study of micro-organisms such as bacteria and viruses. We had thirty-two hours of general microbiology lectures and thirty-two hours of oral microbiology lectures along with twelve hours of an oral microbiology lab. The lab was a big joke. The purpose of one experiment was to see where the highest levels of bacteria were in the Dental Sciences building. We divided into groups of four and each group was responsible for exposing a sterile petri dish for ten minutes in a designated location. We let the plates culture for a week and then counted and identified what grew. One group took their dish into their designated washroom and all four spit on it. One guy from another group even stuck his finger up his ass and then streaked his finger across the dish.

The results were bizarre. The group that had spit on their dish had over thirty different types of bacteria. The guy who stuck his finger up his ass had only twelve different types of bacteria but scored the second highest overall count for number of bacteria. Ironically the highest overall level of bacteria was found in the dental clinic's main waiting room. A type of bacteria that is normally found only in the anus of a duck was also found in the waiting room's sample. Our professor was at a loss to explain the results.

For another experiment we all took swabs from our own mouths and then studied the cells under microscopes. One of the " glamour girls" in our class called an instructor over as she was examining the cells from her own mouth. She was having problems identifying what she saw through the microscope. The male instructor turned bright red after he took a look. Apparently the cell she couldn't identify was a spermatazoa. She'd been at her boyfriend's over the lunch hour just prior to the lab. It didn't take a genius to figure out what happened.

My embarrassing moment came during a general microbiology lecture in November. We were only five minutes into the lecture when I asked Vijay, who was sitting beside me, what kind of sandwich he was eating. Unlike high school it was generally accepted you could eat during lectures in university, as long as you didn't disrupt the class. Vijay jokingly replied that he was eating a whale uterus sandwich. I giggled. I couldn't help it. Although my giggles weren't very loud, Dr Bunj, our lecturer, definitely noticed. The lecture room was designed so the seats were arranged in a semi-circle around the central lectern. We unfortunately had ringside seats. Dr Bunj's style of lecturing was very serious, very dry and very boring. Physically he reminded me of Peter Sellers in The Party. When Dr Bunj noticed me giggling he abruptly stopped lecturing and walked right up to me, his face ending up only inches away from mine. He just stood there for a full thirty seconds and I could feel the tension building. Glaring at me the entire time he finally demanded, "What is so funny that you must disrupt my class?" Not knowing what to say I told the truth. My voice felt as dry as sandpaper when I spoke. "I just asked him", I pointed towards Vijay, "what kind of sandwich he was eating?" Still glaring at me Dr Bunj ordered, I want you out of my class!"

Actually I was hoping Dr Bunj would have followed up on the sandwich thing so Vijay could have said, " whale uterus sandwich" and the whole class could have had a good laugh. Unfortunately Dr Bunj had no apparent interest in the sandwich. Not wanting to suffer the stigma of being kicked out of class I pleaded with Dr Bunj. " I'm sorry, I didn't mean to cause problems. It won't happen again." Dr Bunj seemed unconvinced but said, still not too amiably, "Okay you can stay, but I will not tolerate any further disruptions. Is that clear?" He directed his question to both Vijay and myself and we rather eagerly responded almost in unison, like a couple of village idiots, "Yes sir!" For the rest of the class I almost died from suppressing the violent urge to explode into laughter. If I'd have glanced just once at Vijay I know I would have lost it. To be safe I avoided the remainder of Dr Bunj's lectures.

A definite blow to my self-confidence in second year was my progress in operative dentistry. Instead of Dr Willlis our professor was now Dr Imanka, the chairman of the operative dentistry department. Dr Imanka seemed to come from the same mold as Dr Willis. He was harsh, demanding and unforgiving. All through second year I was terrified and totally intimidated by him. Unfortunately it wasn't until third year that I discovered he was actually a very fair and even kind instructor, underneath his gruff exterior.

Dr Imanka had trained in Japan and still spoke with an accent. His pronunciation of certain words was atrocious. Every time he attempted, "glass ionomer" it sounded like he was saying "grass zoo animal."

Fairly frequently Dr Imanka had most of the class in stitches from his dropped consonants, dropped vowels and magical words. For example, he started one of his lectures, "Dis morning I was in showah and I got haih in my mouth." All I could think of was Dr Imanka with a pubic hair in his mouth. Obviously others in the class had been thinking along similar lines because there were assorted giggles, snorts and outright laughter from all corners of the class. Dr Imanka noticed our amusement and asked rhetorically to no one in particular, "What is so funny? Haven't you had haih in your mouth in showah?" This was of course met with even more laughter. Looking slightly bewildered by all the commotion he continued, "When I felt haih in my mouth I dinking I know haih is only twenty-five micwons wide, yet I can tell deeference with my teeth. This is weason why dentistwy is so pwecise. If you make mistake of only twenty-five micwons you fail." Now that he explained himself the laughter died away.

In Dr Imanka's class I found that drilling and filling didn't come easily to me. Part of the reason may have been that I never, not once, in all of second year operative dentistry, received one single word of positive feedback. Nevertheless I showed my efforts to our instructors again and again and every time I got shot down.

As an example, one day our class was working on drilling out a lower molar. I'd worked for about a half-hour and thought I'd done a pretty good job when I showed my prep to our row instructor. He shook his head and said that I still had to drill down another millimeter. Taking my prep back to my seat I drilled down about another millimeter and showed it to him again. This time he told me in a disgusted tone of voice that I'd drilled a half-millimeter too deep and that if I didn't do another prep to the proper depth he'd have to fail me for the day's work.

The day-to-day assignments and work in operative dentistry were child's play compared to our

practical exams. There were four in total and I always had problems sleeping before each and every one. I thought that as time went by and I became more confident in my abilities the practicals would become less of an ordeal. They told us at the beginning of the year that we needed an overall sixty percent on our four practical exams to pass second year. And because of the dreaded practical exams I had visions of having to repeat second year. It didn't help when I got 57% on the first exam and 58% on the second. Subsequently I was a total basket case before the third exam. I remember Dr Imanka came up to me before the third exam and told me to do well since the results of my first two exams were " not that good." He said it in a joking kind of way but his words did nothing for my self confidence. Up to that point I knew my performance hadn't been spectacular but I didn't know that they knew it too.

Despite the incredible stress I pulled through and ended up getting a 65% bringing my overall average for the three exams to a dazzling 60%. This meant the pressure was still on for the last exam. It was frustrating since most of my classmates who I really hated had a high enough average going into the last exam that they could totally screw up and still pass the year. Maybe part of the reason I hated some of these people was because they never knew what it was like to have to sweat it out. To make matters worse some of the most obnoxious classmates flaunted their marks. I felt like killing the guy who complained loudly that he'd only gotten 78% on the second practical exam. He rubbed it in even more by saying how depressed he was because of his mark.

My friends, with the exception of Dan academically and Vijay handswise, were all in the sweat-it-out category. That's undoubtedly part of what drew us together so closely. We shared the same pressure, the same agony and the same fears. Ultimately we were all afraid of failing and having to repeat a year or, even worse,getting kicked out completely.

Naturally I felt that fear before our last operative practical exam. To make matters worse the exam took place the week before our twenty-one final exams. Worrying about the practical exam only made it more difficult to study for the finals. I can't truly describe the pressure I felt before that last practical exam! There was no room for error.

I needed to get sixty percent or I would fail the year. Our task was to drill an upper first premolar. We were to do an MO prep. That was a two surface prep that included the occlusal surface and the mesial wall. The mesial surface meant that part of the tooth that was closest to the canine tooth. The occlusal surface was simply the central biting surface of the tooth.

I was so nervous that my hands were visibly shaking. I tried to calm myself using deep breathing techniques, but they didn't seem to help. I started drilling. I was doing fine until my hand slipped and my drill chattered right through the wrong side of the tooth. It was an automatic failure. My heart sank. I felt doomed. I knew then, that I was going to have to cheat. I was going to have to unscrew the tooth from the dentoform and put a brand new tooth in.

I looked furtively around to see if any instructors were watching. I opened up my drawer, found the proper replacement tooth and grabbed hold of the screwdriver. Leaning over the dentoform to hide my intent I quickly unscrewed the bad tooth and slipped the replacement tooth in. Just then one of the row instructors came walking by. My heart felt like it was going to bounce out of my chest. He passed me and headed to the front of the class. With my hands still shaking, I screwed the new tooth in and slipped the old tooth into my drawer and closed it. I took a deep breath and felt the panic subside.

I started drilling again, this time I held the drill in both hands so it wouldn't/couldn't slip. I finished the prep to the best of my abilities within the required time frame. I knew my occlusal floor was too deep and it had a slight tilt, but overall I knew it wasn't too bad. They posted the marks fifteen minutes later and I was thrilled to see my mark. Sixty percent. I had passed the practical component of second year operative dentistry.

Removable prosthodontics consisted of two components. Complete dentures and partial dentures. Since we had finished our complete denture before Christmas, it was now time to devote our time to partial dentures. While complete dentures replace all your teeth, partial dentures replace only some of your teeth.

The most critical aspect of partial dentures was in their design. Basic physics was the guideline to most designs. You never wanted to put too much strain on the existing teeth. As well, the added teeth needed to be stable under severe chewing conditions. There were two main types of frameworks. Acrylic or metal. Each had inherent advantages and disadvantages which were unique to each and every case.

Before we started any actual lab work,-we were given what felt like hundreds of cases to design. It was frustrating because some of the designs went against the laws of physics. When I asked Dr Keller why these designs worked he simply said, " I don't know."

That's what consistently disappointed me about dental school. You were expected to accept what you were taught with dutiful allegiance. Independent thought was totally discouraged and even penalized. I'd asked one of my professors in first year if anyone had ever studied the effect of x-rays on your brain at the exact moment of exposure. He thought about it for a nano-second and replied, "Don't worry ,- it's not going to be on your exam." I didn't care if it was going to be on my exam. I just wanted to know.

When we got around to the lab exercises for partial dentures it was a mess. The impression material we were using had the same consistency of hot molasses. It went everywhere and stuck to everything,- except to where we wanted it to stick. It took countless attempts to get an accurate impression. Dr Keller didn't make it easy for us. If he saw any spilled material on the floor or dental chair, he automatically failed you. To top it off he was notoriously hard of hearing and he had what seemed to be uncontrollable flatulence. Somehow partial dentures had become another one of our nightmare courses.

* * *

In the middle of February I gave my first needle. I'd heard that nurses and doctors practiced giving needles by injecting oranges. Only after they'd perfected their technique on the lowly Sunkist were they allowed near real patients. As brave but naive dental students we skipped the oranges and went right to real people. Unfortunately the people we practiced on were ourselves.

On the afternoon we gave our first injection we were told to pair up and to choose our partner very carefully. After all you didn't want someone that didn't like you coming at you with a needle. With our partners we were supposed to practice two different types of injections-infiltration and block. I knew the theory behind both types of injections. Infiltrations were simple. All you did was stick the needle into the person's gums and inject. A block was more involved. For this type of injection you had to put the needle in and position the tip to the precise location of a major nerve before you injected.

By mutual consent Paul and I became partners. Right from the start I told Paul of my morbid fear of needles. Actually when I consider how afraid I am of getting needles in my mouth it's a wonder I ever decided to become a dentist. Before I was seven years old I wouldn't let my dentist anywhere near my mouth with a needle. I'd open my mouth and hold still only as long as he didn't give me a needle. Eventually, as my cavities got bigger and the drilling really started to hurt I finally consented to my first dental needle. I was nine but I still cried. In fact it wasn't until high school that I could take a needle stoically, without screaming or crying.

When I was in grade twelve I skipped the last of our government mandated booster shots. One minute I was in line, the next I was walking down the hallway in the opposite direction. My fear was so profound that I hid in the washroom for the next half hour.

When I was in my first year chemistry program I donated blood. I had the best intentions, but when they stuck me in the arm with the needle I passed out. I was already lying down so I didn't fall over. My heart was beating so fast I filled the blood bag in about thirty seconds.

Since then I'd been pretty good at avoiding needles. That is, until Paul started coming at me with his shaking hand. I agreed to let him go first so I could get it over with. The plan was for Paul to infiltrate me, then I'd infiltrate him. Then he'd block me and finally I'd block him. When Paul stuck the tip of the needle into my skin I felt a very faint prick. As he injected the local I could feel the area start to numb up almost instantaneously. His hand shook wildly but I didn't care. I had disassociated my body from my consciousness. I pretended I was lying on a beach in Aruba,- soaking up the sun. What was going on in my mouth was far away and distant. When Paul withdrew the tip of the needle from my mouth I returned to the here and now. Looking up at Paul I said, "Hey that was pretty good, I barely even felt it. " Paul looked pleased for a brief moment until he realized it was now his turn.

"Okay, Paul,hop in the chair so I can give you some of your own medicine." I tried to keep the atmosphere jovial. As Paul and I switched places I pondered out loud, hmm.... infiltration looks too easy. Let's go straight for the block. What do you think Paul? "He didn't look too thrilled but I just chalked it up to his being on the wrong end of the needle. "Sure, go for it,-" Paul said with considerably more bravado then enthusiasm. Theoretically I knew how to give a mandibular block but having never actually done one before I was unsure of myself.

As Paul opened wide I felt for the proper landmarks with my left hand. I placed my thumb on the retromolar pad at the back of Paul's mouth, my third finger on the angle of his mandible and my second finger about an inch below his ear. With my right hand I aimed the needle between my second and third fingers and pushed the tip into his gum just past the edge of my thumb. The precise moment the needle penetrated his skin I noticed his eyes flinch. I pushed the needle in about an inch until it hit bone. Again Paul's eyes flinched. I withdrew the needle a fraction of an inch and lifted my thumb from the end of the syringe in order to aspirate. As soon as my thumb came free of the end- the whole syringe slipped from my hand. Almost as if it had a will of its' own it drove forward into Paul's mouth until the needle was buried to the hub. (about two inches) I almost expected to see the tip of the needle come through the outside of Paul's jaw at the back.

His reaction was memorable. He tried to scream but with two inches of hard steel stuck in the back of his mouth, the scream sounded more like a small dog's yelp. As he tried to scream his hands and feet simultaneously flew into the air and his eyes looked like they were about to jump out of their sockets. I pulled the needle out as soon as I regained my grip on the barrel of the syringe. The moment I was clear of his mouth Paul cried out, "Holy shit!!! What happened?" I tried to explain, "I'm sorry Paul, I went to aspirate and I sort of lost control." Paul said, " Yeah thanks numbnuts, tell that to your next patient." He was pissed off. Justifiably so-and jumping at the bit for revenge. That was when I decided it was time to call it quits. I knew Paul wanted blood. Mine. There was no way I was going to let him anywhere near me with anything sharper than a cotton ball. He'd given me one injection and I'd given him one. So we were sort of even.

Trying to keep my rabid fear from showing I explained, "Look, we'll be doing injections for the rest of our lives. What difference does one less make. C'mon let's call it quits. We can go grab a couple beers. I'll pay! " Paul responded, "You're being a suck. I owe you a block." Just then our instructor came by and asked how things were going. Dr Kamp was a heavyset, dark haired professor of oral medicine. He was in his early fifties and reminded me of Fred Flintstone both in physical appearance and with his gruff mannerisms. Before Paul could say anything I spoke up, "Very good, sir, we've just finished." I pointed to my drooping upper lip and gestured in Paul's direction implying that Paul too had suffered the indignities of the exercise. Dr Kamp smiled and walked on.

"Okay Paul, let's get out of here while the goings still good," I suggested, hoping Paul's lust for revenge had diminished. After a thoughtful pause he replied, "You chicken shit, just remember you owe me one."

Ten minutes later Paul and I were lounged out in the student pub staring into full glasses of ice cold Budweiser. It was four in the afternoon but the pub was packed. Must be nice to be a normal student. They probably had no more than twenty hours of classes a week. They had time to sleep in, time to do their homework and obviously they had time to sit in the pub and drink beer at four in the afternoon. They were all around us in their little cliques, pathetically complaining about how tough school was. Yeah, I really felt for them. This was only the second time I'd been to the pub on a weekday.

Immediately to our right was a cluster of five young women all looking as if they'd stepped out of the pages of Vogue magazine. I don't think I'd ever seen so much hair in one spot. Paul was kind of licking his lips and staring in their direction. His love life was like mine at the time. Non-existent. Like me he had expected women to crawl all over him when he told them he was in dentistry. But like me he was finding it didn't get you to first base. At this university you needed to have a name like Buffy or Josh and you needed to have rich parents. At least I'd been to other universities and I knew the gold digger mentality so prevalent here was not universal.

The girls beside us seemed the type. The one closest to us had glanced in our direction for a nanosecond when we first sat down. After that she promptly ignored us. None of the other girls even once glanced in our direction. It was as if the first girl had sized us both up in that quick glance and then secretly communicated our taxonomic classification as non-existent to the others.

Keeping an eye on them I asked Paul, "Who do you hate the most in our class?" "The most?" Paul answered the question with a question. After taking a healthy swig of his Bud Paul responded, "Probably Rob Lerner. " Without prompting he explained, "Rob thinks he's hot shit. He's always buddy, buddy with the profs, kissing their asses. He talks like a queer, dresses like a prep. Yeah definitely Rob." Changing the specific topic but not overall subject Paul asked me, "What about profs? Which prof do you hate the most?" I didn't even need to think about that one. I said, "Dr Willis hands down!" Paul thought about it for a moment, took another big gulp of beer and nodded. "Yeah, I'd have to agree with you.Dr Willis is an asshole,but there are a lot of others."

I'd noticed the girls beside us were all drinking white wine except for one in the middle who was working on a mixed drink of some sort. Thinking what assholes our profs were was getting me depressed. I'd have to change the subject before we'd both be wallowing in self-pity.

"So what's new with Lucy?", I asked. Lucy was Paul's friend with benefits. He met her in first year and they still got together every couple of months. Supposedly she was wild in the sack and Paul usually kept us entertained with stories of her latest sexploits. She worked as a waitress at a greasy spoon restaurant downtown and according to Paul she could suck the chromosomes off a trailer hitch. Unfortunately Paul hadn't seen her for over three months. After a couple more beers we decided to pack it in and head home.

In the last quarter of second year we were each assigned our first real patient. As far as our dental education was concerned it was a milestone. We were to examine our patient's teeth and after a complete oral exam we were to present our findings to an instructor. The last and final clinical exercise in second year was to clean our patient's teeth.

My first patient James was a twenty-one-year-old accounting student. I couldn't have asked for a better patient. When I phoned him to arrange appointment times I was surprised by how young he sounded. He totally rearranged his schedule to accommodate the times I had available. Next year I would discover how rare that was. One of the most unpleasant and frustrating aspects of our clinical years was arranging our patient's appointments. We, the student, were responsible for all the scheduling. There was really no other way to do it with so many students and patients. At times I dreamed of having a private secretary and receptionist.

I had three appointments with James in second year. One to check his teeth. one to have an instructor check my findings and finally one to clean his teeth. The first appointment took over two hours. I spent most of the time just talking with James. It felt odd and exciting to place my mirror and explorer into someone's mouth. My hands felt clumsy and awkward, still very unsure of what to do.

During our second appointment I almost lost it. I was so close to bursting into uncontrollable nervous laughter. What was I supposed to do when Dr Edmund, the instructor, farted out loud? There we were, the three of us in one small cubicle. I'd just presented my diagnosis and treatment plan. James was lying nearly horizontal in the dental chair with Dr Edmund sitting down peering into James's open mouth. I was standing on the opposite side of James, wondering how Dr Edmund ever got to be an instructor or even a dentist, for that matter.

Dr Edmund had a strong Russian accent and she looked like a man. Her short, greasy brown hair covered her head like a kitchen mop. She was wearing dirty clothes that had been stylish about twenty years earlier. Dr Edmund's favorite expression was, "Do you understand?" After everything she asked, "Do you understand?" What I couldn't understand was why she smelled like a bag lady. Obviously she was a well-educated and intelligent lady but somewhere along the way she'd lost the desire to present herself in a feminine manner.

I was leaning over James looking into his mouth when Dr Edmund asked me, "Do you understand?" for about the twentieth time. And then Dr Edmund farted. In the tiny cubicle the sound echoed and then the putrid smell hit me. James was looking at me with an odd expression on his face. Dr Edmund was waiting for me to respond to her question and I was on the verge of losing all control. I avoided eye contact with both of them and said, "I don't know." I bit my lower lip hard and forced myself to listen to Dr Edmund explain the function of the sublingual salivary glands. Somehow I made it through the rest of the appointment.

Right after Dr Edmund left the cubicle James and I took one look at each other and burst out laughing. My last appointment with James went smoothly. He had excellent oral hygiene and there was very little plaque and no tartar to clean off his teeth. I lucked out. Other students spent up to three or four appointments to finish cleaning their patient's teeth. The next time I would see James would be in third year.

In the last quarter of second year we started two new lab courses-One in orthodontics, the other in endodontics. For orthodontics we learned to bend wire. Although it may sound easy bending wire to exact shapes and dimensions, it's actually quite difficult. I failed to see how bending wire accurately would improve our manual dexterity or make us better dentists.

At least our lab in endodontics seemed practical. We were given actual extracted teeth to practice doing root canals on. It gave us a feel for what it would be like to do a real root canal. I guess I didn't take either the wire bending or root canal assignments seriously enough because I ended up failing both. To make matters worse I was the only one in the class to fail both exercises. I think I was the only student in the history of the dental school to fail both.

After meeting with the instructors from both courses they graciously agreed to give me another chance and let me resubmit new assignments. While the rest of the class was studying for the dreaded final exams I had to spend hours in the lab bending wires and redoing root canals. Besides taking away valuable time I could have spent studying it was another punishing blow to my self-confidence.

When they first printed our final exam schedule I thought it was a joke. We had twenty-one exams in less than two weeks. How could I possibly cram all that information into my brain?It was physically impossible. If I was a computer it would be easy to load the study tape before each exam, spew out the necessary information for the exam and then repeat. Ironically enough that was very similar to the method I used to survive the exams. Like a computer I crammed in all the information I could the night before, spit out what I could remember on the exam and then I repeated the cycle again arid again. I took sleeping pills to help me sleep and caffeine pills to wake me up.

I actually started studying in February. I found after you memorized something once it was easier to memorize and recall the second time around. In this way I started memorizing pathology, pharmacology and microbiology three months ahead of time. Other courses I studied by reading, reading and rereading my notes. By sheer repetition and maybe even a little osmosis some of it would have to sink in.

The hunt for old exams from previous years started early as well. You could almost always count on a good thirty percent of exam questions being the same as in previous years so it really paid off to get hold of old exams By late March I'd accumulated a stack of them almost a foot high. I spent over fifty dollars in photocopying.

It was amazing how friendly my classmates became at this time of year. People I'd never talked to in almost two years were suddenly best buddies when they ran into me at the library. Where the previous exams came from was a mystery. Exam booklets were never allowed out of the examining rooms and the exams were never returned to us.

My theory was the faculty secretly released a few old exams so we'd at least get twenty to thirty percent right-. They really didn't want to fail us. Funding for the school of dentistry was provided on a per student basis. Even the loss of one student meant a loss of tens of thousands of dollars to the faculty. So the dean, assistant dean and other administrative personnel wanted us to succeed. Unfortunately the benevolent administrators were outnumbered by the sadistic faculty members who wanted to see us fail. Which was why strategy was so important in studying. Knowing the format of each exam was an important part of the strategy.

Most of the exams had a multiple-choice format. By now I was becoming more proficient at this style because I knew the best way to tackle these questions. First, you always started from the back and worked your way forward. This is because the easiest questions were almost always at the end. Conversely the brain-boggling genius questions were usually at the beginning, to slow you down, sap your confidence, waste your time and prevent you from getting to the easy questions at the end. The first time through an exam it was best to answer only the questions that you knew without having to guess. If you were lucky you'd answer at least half. Next time through you'd tackle the questions you were eighty to ninety percent sure of.

You were always racing the clock and the time remaining had a bearing on your final attack. If you were running out of time it was best to guess on the remaining questions using a preponderance of C's for answers. Unless of course marks were taken off for incorrect answers. In which case it was best to leave the remaining questions blank. I think the faculty knew that as a group we were getting better at multiple-choice exams because they started giving us more short-answer, paragraph-style exams as we started ascending our dental school careers. First year final exams had all been multiple-choice while second year turned out to be two-thirds multiple-choice and one-third short- answer paragraphs.

I looked at the clock. It was nine o'clock Monday morning, the first day of our second year final exams. As I skimmed through the multiple choice questions for paedodontics I wondered if I had taken the same course. Most of the questions seemed to have nothing to do with the content of our lectures or textbook. Why did I even study? A wave of cold frustration passed over me with the combination of lack of sleep, keyed-up tension and residual cerebral fogginess from the sleeping pill I'd taken the night before, I thought about walking out. Getting up, handing my virgin unanswered exam booklet to our paedo prof at the front of the room and never turning back. Forgetting about being a dentist and getting on with my life. I was ready to go beyond the curve of Spee. I looked around the room. Everyone else was reading intently, scribbling madly, totally engrossed in the exam frenzy. I seemed to be the only student not working. What was the matter? Wasn't anyone else finding this exam ridiculous?

Just for a second Dan, two rows to my right, looked up and our eyes met. There was no mistaking the look of disgust and panic as he rolled his eyeballs skyward and exhaled a deep sigh. From that moment on I was okay. I knew I wasn't alone. I tackled each and every question and tried not to panic when I ended up guessing on over half. The exam was ninety minutes long. After forty-five minutes one student, Steve, walked up to the front and handed his exam booklet in. I wasn't even halfway through. I wondered if Steve had given up and just packed it in. He wasn't the scholarly type. Steve admitted afterwards that he went through the exam once, answered what he could, guessed at the rest and then handed his paper in. He didn't see any point in hanging around, trying to answer questions he didn't know .I was impressed with his system until I learned that he ended up failing two of the second year finals.

Unlike Steve, I wrote every exam to the last possible second. If I finished early I used the extra time to check over my answers. The two weeks of exams seemed to last forever. Like a kidney stone there was no recourse but to let the flow of time move painfully forward, obliterating exam after exam, until finally it was over. The only real break in the monotony had been the Saturday night between the two weeks. Paul, Dave, Vijay and myself went to a local bar and all ended up getting pissed drunk. Although depriving us of valuable studying time it was probably more beneficial as a purge for our over-tired, overstressed and overstrained brains.

It was two weeks after our last exam that I received the "Personal and Confidential" letter in the mail. The results of the entire second year were in the envelope ready to shoot me down or make me jump with joy. It could go either way. Mentally I prepared for the worst and cautiously ripped open the end of the envelope. Holding my breath I took out the enclosed letter, unfolded it and started reading.

I'd done it! I'd passed everything. Out of twenty-one courses I even had eight honors. For the rest of the day I was on cloud nine. No supplementals. I could get on with my summer.

Unfortunately I hadn't applied for any summer jobs yet because I had seriously anticipated having to come back and write at least one supplemental exam. In retrospect I should have had more confidence in myself and my abilities.

By the time I applied for summer jobs it was too late. Anything that was halfway decent had already been taken. Even my job from the previous summer had been filled since I hadn't applied by the deadline. I probably didn't try as hard as I could to find work because I knew I needed a holiday. The first two years of dental school had been brutal. I needed time to myself with no set schedules or demands so I could prepare myself mentally for the next two years. Luckily I had the luxury of being able to take the summer off thanks to my parents. They paid for my third year's tuition, living expenses and even spending money. As an attempt at recompensation I repainted the interior of our family home during that summer. It gave me something to do as well as making me feel less guilty for taking their money. My parents supported me not only financially but also emotionally and mentally. They were always there for me. Even if they were a hundred miles away, just knowing that they believed in me made a difference.

Although I'd passed all my second year exams, others hadn't fared as well. I called Paul a couple of days after I got my marks and could tell right away from the tone of his voice when he said."Hi" that something was wrong. "Paul, howzit going?" I asked. His reply was somewhat less than enthusiastic. "Aah, Shitty, did you get your marks yet?" Before I could answer he said, "I have to write supplementals in removable, fixed and paedodontics." I felt bad, almost guilty, when I told Paul I'd passed everything. Quite a few people wrote supplementals that summer. Apparently Marcus had been blasted again. He had to write seven supplemental exams. If nothing else poor Marcus had staying power. He just didn't give up. After all the supplemental exams were written everybody was promoted into third year, even Marcus.

Three weeks before third year started I moved into a new apartment with Dan. He'd found a great two-bedroom apartment in a high-rise building right downtown,and he needed a roommate. From second year I knew that I didn't want to live alone again and from first year I knew the type of people I didn't want to live with. In second year I'd been hanging around with Paul, Chris and Vijay mostly, but Dan had also been a good friend. He took dental school very seriously but he also liked to let loose. I figured he'd have a good influence on my study habits.

Our apartment was on the sixteenth and seventeenth floors. The entrance, along with one bedroom and a small bathroom was on the sixteenth floor. Up a flight of stairs was the main living room, a kitchen, a dining room a second bedroom and a full bathroom. The entire apartment, except for the kitchen and bathrooms, was covered with a lush, buttery-soft wall-to-wall carpet. Our view from the balcony on the seventeenth floor was spectacular. We overlooked downtown. At night time the lights stretched as far as the eye could see. We were close to bars, restaurants, movie theatres and even a fitness club that Dan and I joined. Unfortunately the university was over five miles away. There was an excellent, frequent city bus that whisked us from the front of our apartment to the front of the dental school in fifteen minutes. We were almost always guaranteed a seat because the majority of riders didn't get on until the bus was closer to the university.

When I was at the apartment I felt distanced from the dental school. It was high above and far away from the soon-to-be dreaded clinic and I loved it. Visitors were almost always impressed by the striking layout of the apartment and it's panoramic view. It was too bad we had decorated in classic student style. Our furniture consisted of two mismatched couches, two end tables, three lamps, a kitchen table, three fold-up aluminum chairs, a battered twenty-five inch black-and-white TV and various odds and ends. Of course nothing matched. The couches were so bad that even the Salvation Army refused to take them at the end of fourth year when we were moving out. I still had my futon from first year and I still couldn't justify spending the money for a frame so again I slept on the floor. Dan and I were always buying plants to liven up the place but they never survived long. Neither of us had a green thumb.

I remember sitting on the balcony one muggy evening about a week before third year started. I'd had a few beers and was feeling pretty mellow. But the mellowness couldn't hide my fear.

Third Year

On our first day back from summer holidays we received our clinic orientation manual. The size of a King James Bible, it was filled with rules, regulations procedures and bureaucracy. It wasn't easy reading. The purpose of the manual was to make our transition to the clinic as easy as possible. Our schedule was on the third page. It was brutal. Instead of starting at eight thirty we now started at eight, with a one hour lecture until nine. From nine to noon we had clinic. After lunch we had another lecture from one to two and then clinic again from two to five. Five days a week. The actual time we finished in clinic varied. Occasionally we'd still be working on our patients into the lunch hour and even up to six o'clock during the afternoon clinic. At the end of the clinic sessions we were responsible for doing all our own lab work. And it wasn't unusual to have an hour or two of lab work each day.

This meant for the majority of the year we'd be at the clinic from eight in the morning until eight in the evening. It was a punishing schedule that never relented.

For third year we were given specific clinical requirements to complete. In operative dentistry we were to complete a minimum of seventy-five surfaces of silver fillings, eighteen surfaces of white fillings, one gold inlay and two practical exams. In revovable prosthodontics we were to fabricate one upper and lower complete denture and one upper and lower partial denture.single crown and six successful root canals were the minimum requirements for fixed prosthodontics and endodontics respectively.

We had no specific numerical requirements for periodontics. Instead we were responsible for maintaining the periodontal health of all our assigned patients. In orthodontics we had to accumulate fifty points. For example we received two points for taking upper and lower impressions, six points for an orthodontic consult and four points for solving one of the orthodontic problem box cases. Along with our orientation manual we were each assigned our own clinic cubicle and a list of patients. My cubicle was near the very back of the vast clinic. All together there were over a hundred separate cubicles arranged in four alphabetically designated rows. A,B,C and D. Each cubicle was identical. We all had the same eight-foot by eight-foot space, with a ten-year-old harvest gold colored dental chair, ADEC dental light, dental stool, white storage cupboards, sink and a surrounding four-and-a-half foot tall avocado green wall. It was as if we each had our own little dental office. To maintain the institutional flavor we weren't allowed to put up posters,pictures,plants or any decoration that showed any indication of our individuality.

We would be responsible for maintaining our own cubicle in a clean and tidy appearance at all times. During the first few days of third year we all spent hours organizing and packing our cubicle cupboards with the dental instruments we'd been assigned each year as part of our dental student kits.

My cubicle was third from the wall in Row C, otherwise known as C3. For some reason there was a familiar feeling to the cubicle,almost like a deja vu. Two days later I realized with horror that C3 was the very spot where in first year we'd witnessed the old man wanting to kill himself. I took it as a bad omen.

Beside me in C2 was Dave W . On the other side in C4 was Greg Smith, one of the army guys. My roommate for third year Dan was far away in Row A.

The clinic manual was our guide to unraveling the mysteries of the seemingly hostile clinic. From pages six to twenty the basic day-to-day routine was explained. Each row had a different discipline at different times. For instance, on Monday afternoons residents of A Row could only do operative dentistry, while B Row worked on removable prosthodontics and C row did periodontics. To complicate matters, it was possible to switch rows for a single clinic session but only if there was an empty cubicle in that row. This was not an easy procedure since you also needed three separate signatures,-one from the row and discipline you were leaving, one from the row and discipline you wished to move to and finally one from the clinic director.

For each clinic session we were marked on our performance by our row instructor. We were given either E for Excellent, G for Good, S for Satisfactory or the dreaded U for unsatisfactory. U was considered a failure. The unofficial nickname for students who collected a lot of U's was U-Boat Commander. Marcus was promoted from Commander to Admiral of the fleet by Christmas time.

As well as our regular clinic sessions we also had specific rotations in general medicine, oral surgery, emergency dentistry and pediatric dentistry. For general medicine we had a whole week to observe various departments and procedures at several different hospitals in the city. It was the most popular rotation since all you had to do was show up each day. It was a holiday from the regular clinic for a whole week.

The oral surgery clinic was adjacent to the regular clinic. For a week at a time, four weeks in all ,we watched and/or performed various extractions and surgical procedures. It was also a break from the regular clinic. Pediatric dentistry was the most dreaded of all clinic rotations. It was much worse than the regular dental clinic. Assignments to the pediatric clinic were totally random. There was no apparent logic to scheduling. You could go three weeks without doing the pediatric clinic but then the next week you might have two-three hour sessions in a row. The emergency clinic was another rotation. In third year we only had one week in the emergency clinic.

The biggest pain in the ass during third and fourth year was scheduling our patient's appointments. Most of the patients came to the dental clinic for one reason, and one reason only. To save money. The fees at our clinic were very reasonable. They were about a quarter of the cost of a normal dentist's fees. Officially we were supposed to charge our patients for every procedure. In reality most of us never charged our patients or charged them only a fraction of what we should have. In this way we knew they'd come back and they'd be less likely to cancel their appointments. The clinic administration conveniently looked the other way and subsequently we had financially motivated-patients. Of course we had to charge for major procedures like dentures or crowns because for these procedures there was a considerable cost to the faculty in materials. The administration checked these charges and fees very carefully.

Some of us even helped pay our patient's fees for the major procedures, with the understanding that they were not allowed to cancel any appointments or show up late. I knew one girl who not only paid for her patients' major procedures but she also paid her patients ten dollars for every appointment they showed up. To let her work on my teeth I would have insisted on a hundred dollars an appointment. For Marcus I'd want life insurance.

Looking over my assigned list of patients I wondered what they'd be like. There were ten names on the list with notations beside each name.

Maria Lucas-operative dentistry,Stan Gowocki- 0perative dentistry, Jerry Connors-operative dentistry, Mary Frack-fixed prosthodontics, Vijay Chauhhuri-endodontics, Dorothy East-removable prosthodontics, Bev Harding-operative dentistry, Yvonne Bigoldus-fixed prosthodontics, Anna Brice-operative dentistry, Pat Mccomb-removable prosthodontics.

Before I could actually start operative or other work on these patients I needed a minimum of three appointments,-one for an initial oral exam, one to have the oral exam and treatment plan marked off and one to clean their teeth. Only after a patient's' teeth were cleaned and their oral hygiene was in good shape were you allowed to start operative dentistry, removable or fixed prosthodontics or endodontics. From a holistic viewpoint it made sense but for us it was frustrating. Some of our patients needed an additional three to six appointments before the periodontal department granted approval to continue.

I didn't have my first patients until Wednesday of our week back. I booked Maria L. at 9 am and Anna B. at 2 pm for their initial exams. Maria was not what I'd expected. Over the phone she had sounded old and cranky. When I went to the waiting room I called out her name several times before she acknowledged me. She was a knockout. She had long,dark hair, and a stunningly beautiful face, not to mention a body that would make Viagra obsolete.

As I walked to my cubicle with her a couple steps behind , I noticed half the people in the clinic had stopped what they were doing just to stare. I had to admit I lucked out with Maria. Besides being gorgeous she was also reliable. An added fringe benefit of working on Maria was that most of the instructors were too busy ogling her legs and bosom to pay much attention to what I was doing in her mouth.

My initial oral exam with Maria went well. I was a little tense at first but she was so nice, so friendly and so obviously impressed with me that I couldn't help but pick up some of that confidence. For the exam I took X-rays, probed and picked at her teeth, felt for swollen lymph nodes and closely examined all of her oral cavity including palate, tongue, cheeks and throat.

I wondered if she had a boy-friend. She worked as a waitress at a greasy spoon restaurant in the west end of the city. Four months ago she'd gone to a dentist who told her she had a mouthful of cavities that would cost about fifteen hundred dollars to fix. Since she didn't have dental insurance the dentist suggested she come to the student clinic.

At her first appointment I read her the riot act. I would charge her next to nothing if she showed up for all her dental appointments on time. She was as good as her word. She never missed an appointment and in total I only charged her thirty dollars for about fifteen hundred dollars worth of work.

By the time I was finished with Maria that day, it was only eleven. I searched around for someone to go for a coffee with. Paul, across from me,was lounging in his dental chair, studying his orientation manual. When he saw me he whistled, "Hey Ken, want to give me your patient's phone number? Man is she hot.

I've been waiting since nine for my patient and I'm beginning to think the dipstick is not going to show. There's no answer at his house either."

"Well forget it, let's go grab a coffee," I suggested. It didn't take much arm-twisting and soon we were sitting in the med-sci cafeteria garbed proudly in our spotlessly cleaned white dental smocks.

The dress code for the clinic was strict. We had to wear one of our clinic smocks at all times while working on patients. Furthermore, jeans and running shoes were absolutely Verboten and we were also expected to wear a dress shirt and tie underneath our smocks. The smocks were V-neck cotton pullovers and we were responsible for laundering them ourselves. I had heard of students being dismissed from the clinic for having a dirty smock.

Paul and I talked about the events of the summer and then discussed the inevitable and dreaded clinical requirements. That year Paul, Vijay, Dave and myself became our own self-contained social group. Our friendships were really only a continuation from second year but the new challenges, stresses and problems of clinic life brought us even closer together. We all shared a common hatred of the system and our sadistic instructors. We may not have been the best students academically but we cared for our patients and always treated them with respect and dignity. This was unlike many of our arrogant classmates who considered their patients to be mere sub-classes of humanity.

In third and fourth year we used to eat many of our meals at the hospital cafeteria. Quite conveniently our dental sciences building was connected by a long enclosed hallway to the university hospital. Food at the hospital was cheaper and more nutritious than anywhere else on campus. Instead of fries and burgers they had nutritious full meals like Swiss steak, mashed potatoes, corn and brussel sprouts for $3.85. Especially good value were their breakfasts. (Two eggs, bacon, crispy home fries, toast juice and coffee all for $2.45.) By the middle of third year I was eating most of my meals there. It made sense time-wise, convenience-wise and even economically.

When we stayed late doing lab work we'd often walk over to the student pub and have a couple drinks. The pub was a great spot to unwind, act like a regular student and suck back a few brewskies. It was never quite enough to wash away the stink of the clinic but it helped.

At precisely two o'clock I bravely strode out to the waiting room for the second time that day. I thought my next patient would be young from the sound of her voice on the phone, and this time I was right. Unfortunately I had to wait until two thirty to make her acquaintance. Anna came from a small village over an hour's drive away and her father miscalculated on the driving time. I didn't know it then but Anna would not once, not ever, be on time for any of her appointments. That is if she showed up at all.

I often wonder how Anna is today, if she has any teeth left and how many of my fillings are still there. She was fourteen years old but looked more like eleven or twelve. Every tooth in her mouth had a cavity. I counted up all the possible fillings and she had the potential to satisfy over three-quarters of my operative dentistry clinical requirements. Anna was one of twelve children in a family that was dirt poor. Her clothes were always filthy and ragged and all year she wore the same pants, sweatshirt and running shoes. I felt sorry for her. Anna was a great patient when and if she showed up. The problem was getting her to show up. We only had so much clinic time in which to fulfil our clinical requirements and she ended up wasting a great deal of that valuable time.

But unaware of the future, on my first appointment with her I was ecstatic. Counting the decayed surfaces one by one and tallying them up I came up with the grand total of fifty-two silver surfaces and eighteen white surfaces. I was having visions of completing all my operative requirements before Christmas.

From Anna I would soon learn the most fundamental law of the dental clinic. If something looked too good to be true, it was. There was always a catch.

After escorting Anna out of the clinic I was feeling pretty good. I thought myself to be doubly blessed- first with

Maria(super gorgeous) and now with Anna(super decayed). It took about a day to burst my bubble.

Thursday morning I slept in and missed the eight o'clock lecture. Actually I didn't really sleep in. When my alarm buzzed rudely at seven fifteen I decided my bed was a better place to be than my lecture. I set the alarm for another hour and thus began a ritual that would endure for most of third and fourth year. In fact, altogether I made four, eight o'clock lectures for all of third and fourth year. It's not a record I'm proud of. I just knew my limits and sleeping in for that extra hour was something my body needed.

I booked my next patient, Vijay C. for his oral exam at nine o'clock Thursday. When I got to the clinic just before nine I was being paged over the clinic intercom. "Mister Ken Spaldane, number five, Mister Spaldane number five. I remembered reading in the manual about codes. Unfortunately I couldn't for the life of me remember what number five meant. Hastily I flicked through the pages of my ever present orientation manual to the section on Intercom codes. "Number five-report to the clinic administrator." Holy Shit! I'd heard from some upper year students that the clinic administrator was a post-menopausal bitch who ate students for breakfast. If you got on her bad side you might as well change your name and face.

She had the power. She could take away clinic privileges.. I knocked on her office door hesitatingly, fighting off a momentary spasm of panic, and heard a muffled." Come in." As I swung the door open I felt my heartbeat race. Sitting behind a gargantuan desk was a kindly,looking, little old granny. She seemed more like the fairy godmother than a wicked tyrant.

"Are you Ken Spaldane?",she asked in a surprisingly young sounding voice. Being sure not to look perturbed or too cocky I answered, "Yes, you wanted to see me?"

"Have a seat, Mister Spaldane. She impatiently motioned for me to sit and then she started in a slightly more business like tone of voice. " Mister Spaldane, are you familiar with our D2 computer billing form?" I nodded my head. "Good, now why is it you've forgotten to turn in your D2's for your two patients

yesterday?" She had me there. I had simply placed the D2 billing form in the patients' charts and filed the charts back in the
Administration Central Registry. My voice stammered when I
told her, "Uh, I didn't know we had to return the D2's- I just
left them in the patients' charts." She looked pleased, like she'd
just caught me with my finger up my nose. "Well Mister Spaldane, it's okay this time, but you must realize that to run this
clinic efficiently there are certain rules and regulations that must
be followed. On your way out could you please take your D2's
from yesterday and drop them off in the D2 slot. And Mister
Spaldane," she winked at me,"Good luck this year."

* * *

I couldn't believe it. As I left her office I thanked her and
wished her a good day. She was a teddy bear, not at all the mon-
ster she'd been made out to be. For the next two years I never
had a problem with her. If anything she went out of her way to
help me if I had any administration concerns.

My day went steadily downhill from the moment I walked
out of the administration office. My patient for nine o'clock
didn't show up. When I phoned him he didn't know if he still
wanted to come to the clinic. He was getting dental coverage in
three months and furthermore he complained that he was missing too much time off of work. I didn't argue. I figured there was
no point. I basically agreed with him and wished him luck, trying to sound sincere. Secretly I was hoping for a plague of crabs
to infest his underwear.

It wasn't until later in the year that I learned the art of making patients feel sorry for you and the science of manipulation
by pity. Of course you had to stoop pretty low to resort to the
old pity routine and since this was only the first week of clinic I
hadn't yet reached that level of desperation.

Since I had no patients for the rest of the morning I decided
to return home to sleep. Leaving the clinic I felt a pang of
guilt that lasted all of two seconds. At the apartment I opted
for a little sun-tanning instead of sleeping since it was such a
gorgeous day. I climbed up to the top (twentieth) story of our

building and lay out on the communal terrace. The sun burned down from the high cloudless sky and there was only the faint whisper of a breeze to cool the air. At this height the sounds of the city far below seemed dampened, as if covered by a blanket. I liked to take advantage of nice weather even if the ultra-violet rays were slowly malignantizing every cell in my body. Later in the year I even went once or twice a week to a tanning salon for my five doillar thirty-minute,Club Med fix. It was never enough to give me a tan, just enough to add a little color to my otherwise drab existence. I read somewhere that brief exposure to bright light was being used therapeutically to treat seasonal affective disorder. From my experience I would tend to agree.

The sun seemed to rejuvenate me so when I returned to the clinic that afternoon I was feeling less oppressed. I was also feeling like I would have rather stayed in the sun, but I knew it was important to get off to a good start in the clinic. I thought it would take the pressure off later in the year and even let me partake of the sun's natural radiance again in the spring if I finished my clinical requirements early. (I was still idealistic and naive enough to believe in that possibility.) The reality was a malevolent, hellish existence of staggering proportions. If you made good progress or even started to get a little ahead of the rest of the class you were slowed down, stopped or even sent backwards a few steps. The obstacles were ever present and sinisterly hidden. Administrative setbacks, instructors who treated us like morons, low marks, long hours, rules and regulations, surly uncooperative patients. The list of obstacles was endless and our goal seemed all but unattainable.

That afternoon I saw my patient from second year, James. Although I had cleaned his teeth last May I had to clean them again before I was granted periodontal approval. Once I had the green stamp from the periodontal department I could start fixing James' decayed teeth.

When I saw James in the waiting room I barely recognized him. Wearing an Armani suit he appeared very much the successful young urbanite. Last year while finishing his college course in accounting he'd always worn jeans, sweatshirts and running shoes.

Apparently right after graduation he'd been appointed a fairly high up job in the accounting firm that his wife's father owned. James wasn't the kind of guy to take advantage of his in-laws and I knew he was probably working twice as hard as any of his colleagues to justify his placement. I was happy for him. I was also wondering how long he would stay my patient since he was obviously making good money now. But I didn't have to worry. Not about James anyway. He was one of those one in a hundred patients who never cancelled, never showed up late and would faithfully finish his entire treatment plan with me. On top of that he was a nice guy and very easy to work on. When he opened his mouth, he opened so wide that I thought he would disarticulate his jaw, giving me lots of room for error in manipulating my still inexperienced but cautious drill.

Cleaning his teeth was a cinch. I had cleaned them only five months previously and his oral hygiene was great. Unfortunately I chose Dr Sands as my instructor. I couldn't believe it but Dr Sands refused to grant me periodontal approval. Dr Sands said although I had done a fair cleaning job, he couldn't approve James until he'd seen him again. It was a load of shit. Jame's periodontal condition was stable. James always had good oral hygiene and never had a periodontal problem in his life. Until now.

Little did I know that Dr (Greenlight) Gordon was the second perio instructor working my row that afternoon. If I'd have gone to Dr Gordon instead of Dr Sands I'd have a green perio-approval stamp on James's chart instead of Dr Sands's illegible signature in red ink. It was the first of many strategic errors I would make. After the first week of clinic Dr Gordon always had a long stream of students following him while Dr Sands stood idle. If you saw Dr Sands coming towards your cubicle it was best to hide or look very busy. If worst things came to worst, and he actually started talking to you it was advisable to embarrassingly admit that Dr Gordon was already supervising you.

Luckily Dr Sands was easy to avoid, unlike some of the more malevolent operative instructors.

* * *

The next day I had Maria booked at nine so I could get her initial exam and treatment plan marked off. If I finished before ten I could clean her teeth and get perio approval all in the same morning. To my amazement that's just what happened. Dr Edmund the Russian butch from the previous year's ordeal with James approved Maria's treatment plan and marked me (good) all before nine-thirty. Dr Edmund had no flatulence that morning and only asked me " Do you understand?" about five or six times. I wanted to ask Dr Edmund if she understood what personal hygiene meant or if she herself had used shampoo, deodorant, or soap since I'd last seen her. I knew the answer. As she walked out of my cubicle the acid fragrance of ripe B.O. walked out with her. I was grateful she finished so quickly. So were my overworked olfactory nerves.

Luckily Maria had good oral hygiene because an hour and forty-five minutes later I was ready to get her checked off for perio approval. I waited until Dr Sands was talking on the phone to line up behind Dr Gordon. Ten minutes later I had the green stamp of perio approval and Maria was all set to be drilled and filled next appointment.

At times when my dental mirror and explorer were in Maria's mouth I thought of the famous words of Norm Akado. " Yah fuck, I just pretend my mirror is like, my dick and I move it all around her mouth, Yah fuck, she loves it, man!" Norm was only a year ahead of me in dental school but already a legend to our class. So far he had told Dr Willis to fuck off, right to his face. He had called one of our paedodontic instructors a stupid jerk, again face to face. He also froze up a patient's abscessed tooth so he could polish the filling he'd put in (that had caused the abscess in the first place) and subsequently get operative credits for the polished tooth. This was completely unethical since after the freezing came out the patient was left with a severe toothache. Norm didn't give a shit because he had his operative credits. As an added bonus he ended up with a new root canal case too. The icing on the cake, though, was that Norm took a grade eleven student to one of the dental pubs and got her rip roaring drunk.

That afternoon I was supposed to have Anna's treatment plan checked off. Unfortunately she was a "no show". I waited an hour and a half at the clinic and finally went home feeling both disgusted and secretly relieved. Amazingly she showed up for her appointment a full day late. She called me on Saturday afternoon at two thirty demanding to know where I was and why the clinic was locked. I couldn't believe it. I patiently explained her appointment had been for Friday and she missed it. There was a pause on the end of the line and then she said, "Oh,.... well why can't you see me today?" I could feel myself starting to get angry so in a very controlled tone of voice I told her that the clinic was closed on the weekend and that unless she had a key she was out of luck. She hung up on me. Briefly I thought of phoning her back and giving her shit for not showing up yesterday and for her rudeness today. But I didn't want her mad at me. After all, she had three quarters of my operative clinical requirements in her surly little mouth.

It wasn't until the third week of third year that I did my first filling. Since my lucky number has always been three, the third week seemed an opportune time to begin. Besides, most of my classmates had already finished two or three fillings by this time and I didn't want to get behind the pack.

I couldn't have asked for a better patient for my first filling. Stan was a second year general program college student. He was a couple of years younger than I but looked older because of his majorly receding hairline. Stan's most valuable trait as a patient was his laid- back attitude. I was more nervous than he was. Of course I didn't tell him he was about to be my first filling guinea pig. There were two instructors supervising for operative dentistry that afternoon. The moody and much feared Dr Willis and a woman, Dr Marnie. Dr Marnie was at this point an unknown entity. I chose Dr Mamie as the lesser of two evils. As it turned out I made the right choice. She was nice.

It caught me off guard because I wasn't used to operative instructors showing any indication of warm-bloodedness. Dr Mamie was both warm-blooded and very mammalian. She combined sex appeal with a no-nonsense fairness and nurturing kindness. One of many part-time instructors, she maintained her own private practice and taught at the university for two afternoons a week.

My first filling was to be a two-surface filling on an upper right molar. Once Stan was seated I called Dr Mamie over and told her which filling I wanted to do. She greeted Stan warmly with a throaty hello and had him horizontal all in the space of a few seconds. As she looked in Stan's mouth she leaned over so her left bosom was only centimeters from Stan's face. She poked at the tooth in question, nodded her head at me and said,"Good, call me back after you've anaesthetized and have the rubber dam on." Both Stan and I were in love. After the last hints of her expensive French perfume had dissipated from the cubicle I realized Stan was about to become the lucky recipient of my first real injection. I gobbed lots of topical gel on a Q-tip and explained to Stan that I would be freezing his tooth. I placed the Q-tip in the area where I'd soon be piercing the skin. I left the topical anesthetic on much longer then I needed, stalling for time. As I finally removed the Q-tip from his mouth I warned Stan that he might feel a little pinch at the next part. Stan reached up to scratch the tip of his nose, looked me in the eyes and asked,"Is this the needle?" I replied, "Yeah but hopefully you won't feel a thing. You can close your eyes if you want." I was grateful that Stan took my advice and closed his eyes because that way he couldn't see how much my hand was shaking.

I remember looking at the firm pink texture of the gum and thinking I couldn't possibly stick the super sharp tip of the needle into the skin. It was too gross. My hand was shaking and I felt like puking. Biting my lower lip hard I willed my hand to act. In thirty seconds it was all over. I pulled the needle tip out of his skin, observing the little bubble of liquid that had formed at the injection site. "You can open your eyes now." I said to Stan. His first comment was, "That wasn't too bad."

My next task was to place the rubber dam. I gave the tooth five minutes to freeze up before I started and then spent thirty minutes getting the darn thing on! I knew now why they were called dams. Dave W. helped me with the final positioning. Otherwise it would have taken at least another fifteen minutes. Later that afternoon I helped Dave in placing the rubber dam on his patient. We didn't have to think about helping each other. Right from that first afternoon it was an unwritten, unspoken rule, to always help each other out.

Dave eventually became my best and closest friend. There on the battle lines of the clinic floor our friendship first began and then flourished. I knew I could always depend on him to help me out and vice versa.

* * *

I think what brought Dave W. and I so close together was a feeling of kinship in not belonging. Dave's dad was ethnic Chinese but his mother was from Tibet. His mother's father was Scottish and as a result Dave was six feet, two inches tall. Dave was born in Canada so he didn't really fit in with the Asian culture. And because of his appearance he didn't feel he was accepted as a Canadian. Some people would call Dave a banana, yellow on the outside, but white on the inside.

I loved the way Dave used the English language. You would never know that it wasn't his native tongue. He was brought up speaking Mandarin and he only learned English from watching cartoons on TV and then from school.

I still remember when we were talking about our future. He prefaced the topic with, "Is our future determined by intention or design?" He had a mind that went from A to Z without having to go through B, C, D, etc. We even had our own private jokes. When we greeted each other it was always, "Hey, howzit hanging?" Responses varied according to our moods. "Straight down." "Shriveled and a little to the left." "Tired and to the right." "Smart casual."

One thing Dave W. and I really liked to do was late-night bowling. Typically we went from 1 am to 2 am. Usually we had the place to ourselves. When other people showed up they were most often weird or whacked out, or both,which made the bowling even more fun. I beat Dave almost all the time, but we weren't very competitive. It was more just a different way to work out the stress and tensions of school.

Sometimes Vijay, Paul or Barb would play with us. We always ended up laughing so hard we couldn't really finish our games.

But when it came to the clinic we learned to watch each other's back. If we were working on a patient and we needed assistance, the other person always helped.

Once the dam was on properly I looked around for Dr Mamie. There was a line-up of five students behind her so I took my place and ten minutes later she inspected my rubber dam placement. She said it was good. I couldn't believe it. I'd just received more praise in the last forty-five minutes than I had in the previous two years of dental school.

It was now three o'clock and I was ready to drill. I put my burr in the high speed drill-,gave it a few warm-up whirrs and started very cautiously drilling away on Stan's tooth. It was great for the first couple of minutes until Stan abruptly moved his head to the side and grunted a muffled " nunrumph. " I asked, "Stan did that hurt? Do you need some more freezing?" He nodded his head up and down. To give Stan more freezing I had to remove the rubber dam entirely. By the time I injected and put the dam on again it was three thirty and I was starting to feel anxious. I wasn't sure I would finish in time. Trying to ignore the clock I continued drilling. I discovered that drilling on a real tooth was a totally different experience from drilling on the fake dentoform teeth we had worked on up to that point. As I removed the decayed tooth structure from Stan's tooth I marvelled at how easy it was to control the dental drill. To drill away tooth structure on a real tooth you had to press fairly hard. In contrast the dentoform plastic teeth had been so soft that the faintest caress of the dental drill left an indelible mark on the tooth. I was still drilling away at four fifteen when Dr Mamie came into my cubicle to check my progress. After looking at the tooth she said I was doing a fine job but since we were running out of time I should just put a temporary material in the tooth and I could finish the filling another time. I felt my stomach sink as I envisioned a failing mark.

I followed her instructions, the whole time feeling like a doomed man. After placing the temporary material in the tooth I called Dr Marnie back to have a peek. She snuck a cursory glance, and told me to take the dam off, make sure the bite was okay and call her back for a final check off. By that time my stomach was churning since I was certain she was going to fail me.

At. the final check off she handed me my mark card for the day. I couldn't look. Stan had his mouth open for almost three hours and I hadn't even finished the filling. Actually Stan seemed none the worse for the experience. He thanked me and wanted to know when his next appointment was. As I walked him out of the clinic he asked if Dr Marnie would be there next time. I told him I hoped so. He grinned lopsidedly since the right side of his mouth was still frozen and thanking me again, walked out of the main clinic door with a final wave.

Back in my cubicle I sat on the still warm chair and felt like crying. Not wanting to prolong the agony any longer I finally flipped over my mark card. S+ (satisfactory plus) I almost went into shock. I had actually passed.

That weekend I celebrated by getting drunk both Friday and Saturday with two separate female friends. My personal life had really picked up since the end of second year. I was now dating three separate girls. It was easy to keep them apart because two were from out of town. The girl

I'd dated seriously just before I started dental school, Kareena, called me during my second week of third year. She broke up with her boyfriend and wanted to see me again. I happily agreed to getting together. I still lusted after her but refused to let my emotions carry me away. I figured if she dumped me once she could just as easily do it again. So I put my emotional defenses up and didn't let myself fully trust her. In the first half of third year she came to visit almost every second weekend.

She lived about eighty miles to the east and took the train when she came. I thoroughly enjoyed her visits because I temporarily forgot about my patients and the clinic. Besides she was beautiful and had an almost perfect body.

I met Sue during the summer between 2nd and 3rd year while I was visiting my parents. She worked as a life insurance underwriter at a local insurance company. Right from the start, after meeting at a bar we hit it off. She was recently divorced and while I was with her I didn't think about the clinic at all.

The third girl I was seeing that fall was a third year arts major I met at a party in August. Primarily Anne was at university to get her MRS degree but she hadn't had much luck meeting guys in her first two years of university. In fact I was the first guy in two years to ask her out. It was probably due to the fact that she was maybe thirty pounds heavier than ideal. I didn't care about her weight because she was a very attractive blonde with a great bubbly personality. When I was with her I had a great time and she could easily out-drink me. I loved sleeping over at her house because she had this great wavy waterbed.

She really was a sweet girl.

During the week I concentrated on dental school and during the weekends I concentrated on the girls. It let me stay sane. The clinic was incredibly stressful and the girls were a perfect antidote to the stress. Psychologically I was getting better at disassociating my school life from the rest of my life.

The following Monday after my first filling I booked a thirteen-year-old girl for an orthodontic consultation. At this stage I still thought I might actually learn something about orthodontics in dental school. God knows our orthodontic lectures in second year had been practically incomprehensible. The gist of what we had learned so far was that if someone had crowded or crooked teeth you referred them to an orthodontist.

That morning I had the dubious pleasure of meeting the chairman of the orthodontics department, Dr Heath. I presented my consultation to him. To say he was not impressed would be an understatement. Dr Heath resembled Lurch from the Munster family. Well into his sixties and over six-and-a- half feet tall he loomed over everything and everyone like a staggering white topped vulture. He spoke in a scratchy voice with whistles after every "w" or "s" sound.

After I presented my consultation he transfixed me with his scaly eyes and grinned a little tight half smile. Ah, he liked my presentation, I remember thinking. The first words he said were "How did you ever get to third year?" I felt sick. He proceeded to ream me out verbally for the next fifteen minutes. He wanted to take me up to the Dean and confirm that I really was a third year student. He wanted to see me back in second year or preferably not in dentistry at all. I was totally unprepared for his wrath.

My problem was I hadn't filled out the standard orthodontic consultation form #36B. This was because I'd slept in for the lecture and I didn't even know of the existence of form #36B. I admitted I must have missed the lecture in orthodontics where clinic protocol was explained to us. He softened a little at the admission of my guilt. Instead of a 1500 word essay I only had to write a 1000 word essay on The Importance of Protocol, to be delivered to his office next Monday morning by nine o'clock.

After that morning I avoided Dr Heath at all costs. Luckily our distaste seemed mutual and I think he did his best to avoid me as well. He wasn't a true sadist like some of the operative instructors who did their best to make you miserable.

That afternoon I was afraid of a similar experience in operative dentistry. I was doing a three-surface filling on one of Maria's upper premolars. My instructor was none other than Dr Imanka, the chairman of the operative department. I was scared shitless. I knew from the first moment Dr Imanka saw Maria I had nothing to worry about. Dr Imanka loved women. Plain and simple. The more attractive or curvaceous the woman, the more he liked them and the more friendly he was. When he strolled into my cubicle to approve my treatment he took one look at Maria and his face curved into an ear-to-ear super grin. Formal introductions seemed to be in order."Maria, this is Dr Imanka." "Dr Imanka, this is Maria." Dr Imanka looked like a little boy in a candy store with a twenty-dollar bill. When Dr Imanka had

Maria open her mouth he put his mirror inside but his eyes were on her breasts.

"Ah, very good. You may begin. Call me if you have any questions." His tone of voice was a gentle caress and I felt my tension level drop a notch or two. Every five or ten minutes Dr Imanka came to check my progress. It was almost like I had my own private instructor. I don't think he ever once really looked in her mouth. Instead he was looking at her breasts each time from every angle possible. She was wearing an ivory white fish-net sweater that afternoon and I had moved the dental bib as low as it would go to reveal more of her considerable cleavage. The resultant firm and gentle swell of golden brown skin where the two breasts met in glorious harmony was my ticket to a good mark.

Compared to my first filling with Stan everything went much smoother and faster. I was finished by four thirty and Dr Imanka gave me an overall G (Good). I wasn't sure if he had actually looked inside her mouth. I made a mental note to myself to book Maria on Monday afternoons when Dr Imanka was instructing.

Next morning Anna my fourteen-year-old nightmare patient failed to show up again. In frustration I called her that evening and laid down the law. If she cancelled one more time without twenty-four hours' notice I would have her kicked out of the clinic. For all I cared her teeth could rot right out of her little head. Furthermore she was not to be late for any future appointments or same thing, expulsion from the clinic. She started to cry, which made me feel like a shit. But only for a second or two. It was either her or me and I wasn't about to let a fourteen-year-old snot-nosed brat who lived on potato chips and pop, get the best of me. I relented a little by saying it was alright if she was late up to twenty minutes because I knew she came from far away and it was difficult to predict road conditions. She stopped sniffling and we set up her next appointment.

Probably the reason I was so nasty with Anna was because I was in a lousy mood thanks to my dental patient from that afternoon. Although Dorothy was only twenty-five she needed dentures. She had all her rotten teeth taken out five years earlier and had been saving her money since so she could buy herself a set of dentures.It hadn't been easy for Dorothy. Her family was no help and she was on permanent disability insurance because of a bad back. Social assistance had finally agreed to pay for her dentures as long as she came to the university dental clinic to have them made. Which was how I met Dorothy. I had no idea that people like her even existed. After her first appointment I began to understand the expression- " Room Temperature IQ" Poor Dorothy. Like Cliff Robertson in Flowers for Algernon I hoped she would never have a flash of insight or intelligence that revealed the depressing and hopeless existence of her life. As it was she seemed almost content with the way life had treated her. She would never marvel at the beauty of Beethoven's Ninth or even wonder at the intricacies of a snowflake. Her brain just wasn't wired that way.

Hopefully, by making her a set of dentures her life could be enriched to the extent that she could interact more confidently with other people and eat more solid food. More important to me was fulfilling half of my third year clinical requirements in removable prosthodontics by making her dentures. It was hard to believe but for the previous f ive years Dorothy had been eating with no teeth. Her gums had become as tough as belt leather and she had no problem eating corn on the cob and even steak. I couldn't imagine she had the resources to have steak very often unless it was tube steak.

That afternoon I tried to take a final impression of Dorothy's edentulous lower jaw. Unfortunately the smell of the impression material made Dorothy retch. Every time I put a full impression tray in her mouth she vomited before the impression material had a chance to set up. The first time she caught me by surprise. I no sooner had placed the tray in her mouth when she gagged once and then projectile spewed a vile stream of rose colored barf all over me, herself and the side of the dental chair. I felt myself gag and I almost added to the mess by barfing myself. I pulled the tray of unset impression material out of her mouth and brought her over to the sink to let herself get cleaned up. I glanced down at my clinic smock. The very repugnant puke had soaked through to my shirt underneath and there were little noodle letters of the alphabet clinging to my smock. Apparently all she'd eaten that day had been a bowl of Campbell's Alphabet Soup. Trying to make sense of the letters I imagined a cryptic message forming from the random splatter. Something like, HELP ME or OH MY GOD.

After I cleaned myself off I mopped up the barf on and around the dental chair with paper towels. Dr Keller, our instructor for the afternoon, came over just as I was finishing the clean-up and asked, "Having problems?" Trying to keep a serious face I replied, "Dorothy doesn't like the impression material. We had a bit of an accident." Dr Keller nodded knowingly. I thought I saw a faint smirk at the corner of his mouth. He suggested getting some air freshener from the dental stores.

I tried three more times that afternoon to take an impression and each time I was rewarded with fresh puke. The amount became smaller and smaller each time and by the last impression she was having dry heaves. In disgust I sent her home. I warned her not to eat or drink anything before her next appointment. Even Dorothy's normal bovine complacency had been affected by her excessive vomiting. To add insult to injury Dr Keller failed me for the day's performance.

He strolled into my cubicle while I was swabbing down my dental chair with bleach. Dr Keller never looked directly at your face as he talked. Instead he addressed my legs, somewhere around the knees." Ken, I'm sorry but I have to give you a failing grade for today's work." I had a silly urge to ask him if he liked Alphabet Soup. Dr Keller continued working his way up to my torso with his eyes. " I don't think you handled the situation in a very professional manner." He was probably referring to the time he saw me imitating Dorothy's gagging behind her back. I was driving Vijay, whose cubicle was across from mine, into hysterics, Of course I had no idea Dr Keller would be looking at that precise moment. If Dr Keller had a sense of humor he probably wouldn't have failed me. I might as well have wished for Christmas in July

That night I dreamt of Dorothy. She was explaining the theory of relativity while eating corn on the cob with her gums.

When I started talking to her, she started puking alphabets all over me. When I awoke to the harsh buzzing of my alarm clock I hit the snooze button, reflected a moment on my bizarre dream and decided to forgo the eight o'clock lecture once again. Sleeping in was starting to become a habit.

That morning I started my first root canal. The patient, Vik, was a Pakistani man in his early forties. The only reason he came to the clinic was to save money. Vik whined and complained from the moment he sat down until he left each and every appointment. Initially he was thoroughly disgusted when I told him the root canal would take either three or four clinic sessions to finish. To make matters worse Vik smelt like he hadn't washed in months. He always had tiny, white scaly flakes in his hair and the longest nose hairs I had ever seen.

My instructor that morning, Dr Kocher, was an endodontist who worked part-time at the university to get his jollies. Dr Kocher was an angry man. Although he probably grossed over half a million a year he wasn't very happy because his ex-wife got a big chunk of that and the government got almost all the rest. He probably ended up with just enough to make payments on his BMW. Dr Kocher was like the smart aleck brat who sat behind you in grade ten and constantly whipped spitballs at the back of your head.

After that morning I didn't know who I disliked more, Vik, or Dr Kocher. I thought I did well for my first root canal. Vik was difficult to freeze and I made him grunt in pain three times until Dr Kocher, fed up with my efforts, executed the coup de grace. He shot freezing right down the still vital root of Vik's tooth. At that precise moment Vik did more than grunt. He let loose a blood-curdling scream only slightly dampened in clarity and volume by the rubber dam. Even Dr Kocher seemed a little frazzled. After that things went smoothly and at ten to twelve I put a temporary filling in the tooth and asked Dr Kocher to check things. He begrudgingly gave me a passing mark but commented on my failure to provide adequate anesthesia for the patient.

I decided not to work with Dr Kocher in the future if I could avoid him. It turned out to be a wise decision. One morning Dr

Kocher failed every single student he was supervising. There was a rumor he was dumped by his girlfriend the night before. I think he was a miserable SOB in general and didn't need an excuse to be mean. His specialty, endodontics, was one which most likely did not cultivate personality and good naturedness. Imagine, almost every patient you dealt with was in pain. I think that after a while it would get to you.

That afternoon I paid my first visit to the pediatric clinic, otherwise known as SPEC

(Simulated Practice Environment Clinic). Being on the third floor of the dental sciences building it was removed from the main clinic downstairs. All together the SPEC had eight separate dental cubicles. They were more modern and spacious then our own cubicles downstairs. In SPEC we had the opportunity to practice four-handed dentistry. We were each assigned a dental assisting student to help with our patients. Although generally being nice to look at, the assistants were usually worse than useless. Most of the time you could grab a dental instrument yourself, much easier and faster than by asking the dental assistant to hand it to you.

My first afternoon in SPEC passed relatively uneventfully. I did a check-up and cleaning on a six-year-old boy who was very well-behaved. My clinical instructor Dr Pitts made me redo the cleaning three times before he was satisfied with the end result. Dr Pitts looked like a kid himself, being quite short in height and small in build. It was rumored that he bought his clothes in the children's section at Sears. He hopped around the clinic flirting with the assistants, joking with the kids and always smiling. He had a totally non-threatening manner that gave the clinic an overall relaxed mood. Almost all the other instructors in SPEC were dental student nightmares.

My next session in SPEC was two weeks later. Dr Yank and Dr Flood were the tag-team instructors for the afternoon. Dr Pitts was nowhere to be seen. From a distance Dr Yank and Dr Flood looked almost identical. They were both over six feet tall, slim almost to the point of gauntness with short brown hair and acne-scarred faces. Dr Flood had emigrated from South Africa while

Dr Yank had been educated in Columbia. Simply to look at either dentist was to know fear. Dr Flood cornered me the moment I walked into the clinic. Piercing me with his sun-drenched apartheid icy blue gaze he asked me if I'd read the SPEC orientation manual. I had glanced through it a couple of weeks before so I answered, "Yes, I've looked through it." Detecting the slight hesitation in my voice he started interrogating me. "What is the first thing you must do when you walk into the SPEC clinic? " He had a harsh guttural way of talking which reminded me of Nazi SS officers in old world war two movies. Thinking furiously I tried to come up with the right answer. I finally admitted, "I'm not sure."

* * *

His face broke into a toothsome smile that seemed totally incongruent with the malevolent gaze of his eyes. "Aah, then you haven't read your orientation manual after all? Have you?" Sheepishly I confessed, "I read it a few weeks ago and I might have forgotten some of it." Just then another third year student walked into the clinic. I could see that Dr Flood's attention was now divided between his new potential victim and myself. Before the new student could get far away Dr Flood ordered me, "I'd like you to get your orientation manual and then bring it back here." His condescending manner made me feel like a naughty grade schooler.

I marched out of SPEC and was halfway to my locker before I realized with a sinking feeling in my gut that my SPEC manual was at home. Heading to the main clinic instead I hoped I could find someone who could lend me theirs'. Lucky for me Dave W. had his manual in his dental cubicle. Thanking Dave profusely I headed back up to SPEC with the manual tightly grasped in my right hand. My whole journey had taken about five minutes, but when I got back, Dr Flood was nowhere to be found. In fact I didn't see him again until an hour later. It didn't really matter because where Dr Flood had left off, Dr Yank started.

My patient that day was a four-year-old girl, Tess, who'd never been to the dentist before. My dental assistant had already

104

brought Tess to our assigned cubicle and had her seated by the time I arrived. On my way to the cubicle I was intercepted by Dr Yank. "You're Late!"He barked, pointing to the clock. Very nice to meet you too,I thought. It was probably useless trying to explain that originally I had been on time until Dr Flood had sent me out on a quest. When I tried to explain I realized I was wasting my breath. Instead of being sympathetic he too gave me a hard time about the orientation manual.

* * *

Finally after berating, insulting and generally humiliating me, he let me start with my patient. The check-up with Tess went really well until Dr Flood came to check my progress. Tess took one look at Dr Flood and burst into tears. No matter what he said or did she wouldn't stop crying until he left the cubicle. How did this guy ever become a paedodontist? Later on that afternoon I over-heard Dr Yank and Dr Flood talking together. They were a couple cubicles away from me so even with straining my ears I could only detect bits and pieces of their conversation. I heard Dr Flood say something about a clinic orientation manual and then the phrase, "shouldn't even be in third year." As he spoke these words both members,of the dynamic duo turned simulta-neously and looked right at me. Quickly I turned away. If only I'd read the fucking manual!

Later I learned that Dr Flood and Dr Yank were two of the most hated of all our instructors. The best way to deal with them was to avoid them. Why make life difficult for yourself if you didn't have to? It was only rarely that they both instructed together. If you knew ahead of time that they were both there it was best to be sick and not even show up. More commonly Dr Flood and Dr Yank were paired up with a more benevolent instructor and in these cases it was wise to go to the other instruc-tor right from the start.

Unfortunately I learned the hard way. I didn't get out of SPEC that afternoon until five thirty, long after my patient had left. Dr Flood made me stay late to-,in his words, "contemplate my future." I spent the time planning a double homicide.

Every time we went to SPEC we were faced with uncertainty. Uncertainty with respect to instructor, patient and procedure. Usually a sheet was printed and posted the day before which listed the instructor's names and what procedures each student would be performing on which patient. If you wanted you could alleviate most of the uncertainty by looking at the list the day before. Depending on how you felt about it this was either a benefit or a curse. For example if you saw on the list that Dr Flood and Dr Yank were instructing and you were supposed to do two fillings on the child from hell you'd be up all night worrying. In a situation like this it probably would have been better to not know ahead of time what you were in for. After all, ignorance is bliss.

Besides the instructors the other stressful aspect of SPEC was the patients. All of them were between the ages of three and twelve. Generally the older the patient, the better behaved they were. Naturally there were exceptions.

One afternoon I had to carry a ten-year-old boy, who was kicking and screaming the whole time, from the waiting room to the dental chair. I'd tried every trick I knew to get the brat to come willingly. Mike had been sitting on the waiting room floor right at his mother's feet, happily coloring a Murphy the Molar worksheet. After I said,"Hi Mike" he looked up at me for just a second and then proceeded to ignore me. He focused all his attention on his frantic shading of Murphy. I said, "Hi" again a little louder and then,"Mike it's time for your check-up, would you like to come with me?" As soon as the words came out of my mouth I realized my mistake. I wasn't supposed to ask, I was supposed to tell. Of course he said, " NO!"I would have too if I was in his shoes. Meanwhile his mother was looking a little embarrassed and she tried in a calm, quiet tone of voice. "Mike, I want you to go with the dentist so you can get your teeth checked." And then after a short pause she added, "Right now!" in a loud enough and harsh enough manner that Mike stopped what he was doing and looked up. So did everybody else in the waiting room.

Good, I thought, we've got his attention. "Mike," I tried again in a more assertive manner,"It's time for your appointment. Come with me." I held out my hand to him and instead of taking it he scuttled back along the floor and hedged up right beside his mother. He looked up at her and said in a little sucky boy voice. "I don't want to go, Mommy, I don't want to go. It's gonna hurt!" Looking even more embarrassed by now, his mother avoided eye contact with me and gently but firmly told him, "Mike you have to get your teeth checked. Now go with the dentist right now." Mike started crying and clutched desperately at his mother's leg. "I don't wanna go, I don't wanna go, I don't wanna go," he started chanting. "He's not even a real dentist,Mommy,"he added defiantly.

I tried to remember what our manual said about cases like this. By this time all eyes in the waiting room were focused on us. I grabbed Mike's arm and started pulling him. I had his one arm but he was still clutching his mom's leg with the other. She looked like she wanted to crawl into a hole and disappear. Mike was warming up his lungs with, "You're hurting me, you're hurting me, Oww!" Using a firm but steady pressure I pulled him off his mom. Though he only weighed about eighty pounds he was putting the brakes on with both feet. Getting tired of his antics I finally just lifted him and carried him in my arms. As I was taking him through the main door into the clinic he managed to grab hold of the door frame with both hands. He was yelling at the top of-his lungs, "Mommy! Mommy! Mommy!"

Eventually he lost his grip on the doorframe and I carried him right to the operatory and none too gently I dropped him in the dental chair. I held both his shoulders down with considerable pressure, looked him right in the eyes and spoke loud and clear, "LOOK ! THAT'S ENOUGH!" He seemed momentarily stunned. I think the shock of getting jolted down in the chair had struck true fear into his little heart. From that moment on he started behaving. Maybe he wasn't the greatest but he was at least manageable.

He let me complete the check-up without crying once and with only a minimum of hassle. I think part of the reason he settled down was because his mother was in the other room. A lot of kids will put on a show on for their parents. In class they taught us that poor behavior was often an attention seeking play. In Mike's case his parents were separated and he only saw his mother two days a week. It all made sense.

About a month later I had my worst run-in yet with Dr Yank. I had started the afternoon clinic session with Dr Pitts. My patient was a well-behaved seven year old girl, Sally, and I was sealing off four of her permanent molars with a plastic coating. The rationale behind the procedure was, if you covered all the cracks and fissures on a tooth's surface with a preventative coating then the tooth shouldn't get cavities.

I'd finished sealing both of Sally's lower molars when I noticed Dr Yank glaring over the edge of the cubicle. At that point I wasn't worried because Dr Pitts was supervising me. It had taken careful maneuvering to get to avoid Dr Yank initially. In fact I had a pretty tense few minutes when I first walked into the clinic and only Dr Yank was around. I had turned back out of the main doors of the clinic and sat in a nearby washroom for five minutes. When I returned to the clinic Dr Pitts had appeared so I snuck into my cubicle and ducked every time I saw Dr Yank. Dr Pitts eventually walked by. I snagged him, feeling a vast sense of relief.

But meanwhile Dr Yank was still standing outside my cubicle. He continued to glare. When he started to speak I felt shivers run up and down my spine. "You should be using rubber dam for this procedure." Trying not to appear worried I replied, " Dr Pitts said it was okay to do these without a rubber dam, since the teeth haven't erupted far enough to get the rubber dam clamp on" "Hogwash!",countered Dr Yank, and before I could bring out a silver cross to keep him at bay he was beside me, looming menacingly over pooor, little Sally. He pulled out a rubber dam clamp from one of the drawers and jammed it roughly over one of Sally's upper molars. The sharp metal wings of the clamp cut into Sally's gums and she cried out in pain and shock. "Here, this is how you do it." He was talking to me like I was a retarded kindergarten student. " I want you to use the rubber dam for the other three sealants and I want you to show me the rubber dam when you have it set up for each tooth."

Sally's crying had changed to a dog-like whimpering. When Dr Yank removed the clamp from Sally's tooth, blood literally poured out from where the sharp edge of the clamp had lacerated her gums. Dr Yank stormed out of the cubicle before I had a chance to protest.

I spent fifteen minutes trying to get the rubber dam clamp on Sally's other upper molar without pinching her. Eventually I gave up and reluctantly called Dr Yank over. I told him I couldn't get the clamp on without pinching the gum and he said, " That's not true. You're lying to me." Lying? Why would I be lying?

Dr Yank came back to the cubicle and again he grabbed the rubber dam clamp and brutally clamped it on Sally's tooth. It was obvious from Sally's scream that he had hit her gums. "There," he said, giving me a withering look as if to say," There you stupid moron!" He took the clamp off and said, "Okay, now you try." For the life of me I couldn't do it. Every time I positioned the clamp it looked like it was going to dig right into her gums. On top of that my hand started to betray me by shaking in nervousness.

Without a word Dr Yank grabbed my hand in both of his and roughly positioned the clamp over Sally's tooth. Squeezing my hand in an iron grip he forced me to place the clamp so it closed tightly, visciously into her gums. "Good, now you've got the idea," he explained triumphantly. Yeah I thought to myself, listening to Sally's sobs. Now I know how to torture little girls.

After Sally left, Dr Yank really put me through the wringer. He cornered me in the cubicle as I was cleaning up and he abruptly asked," Mr Spaldane, how thick is the average sealant?" "About a half millimeter?" I ventured in response. Treating me like a cornered rat he laughed mockingly, "About a half millimeter, hmmm...? Is that your final answer?" I felt like taking my fist and slamming it into his leering face, "No, asshole, that's my final answer!"

I answered, "Well I think the average thickness will vary according to the depth of the crack the resin is filling." Dr Yank's smile faded into a caustic slit and he verbally attacked. "No, Ken, you are thinking too much. If you read your manual you would know the average thickness of the sealant. " I couldn't believe it, the fucking manual once again. Obviously Dr Yank had a thing for his precious manual. Continuing his questioning Dr Yank asked "How about an enamel rod? What is the thickness of an enamel rod?" I sheepishly admitted. "I don't know." He withered me further with a look of such disgust and disdain that I felt about two inches tall.

"You don't know?" He roared in triumph "What do you think will happen when you have a patient sitting in the chair and you have to tell them that you don't know? The rest of the clinic was unusually quiet and I realized we'd become the center of attraction. Knowing my predicament was public made the experience even more humiliating. Not knowing the answer to his last question I just sat there looking at the mosaic like pattern on the tiled floor.

"Okay, Ken, I will answer the question for you. The sealant coating is twenty-five microns and an enamel rod has an average diameter of half a micron. What a stunning revelation, I thought to myself. I had to endure another ten minutes of further humiliation until I was finally freed. I vowed to read the entire orientation manual from cover to cover as soon as I was home. I also vowed to avoid Dr Yank at all costs in the future.

A couple of days later I met Dr Yank's counterpart in the main clinic. I'd signed into A row to continue my operative work since I was falling behind in that discipline. The instructor for that afternoon was Dr Guest, with whom I'd never worked with before. Dr Guest was another part-time instructor who only came to the clinic one afternoon a week. He was well over six feet tall but he had a gaunt, stooped-over shape which made him appear shorter. His face looked boyish, almost like Linus from the Peanuts comic strip. But when he moved his mouth or his eyes, all his wrinkles transformed him into an old man. Though he was only in his early fifties he looked much older. The fact that he was almost bald and had a bad comb-over didn't help.

Dr Guest would become the instructor I hated and feared the most. He was the granddaddy of them all. Dr Guest used to stand at the front of a row and talk loudly to the other instructors. Typically it was about how lousy the students were. He'd say things like, "These kids make me sick. I could finish the whole row's work in less then an hour."

One afternoon while he was standing right over my cubicle he carried out a conversation with another instructor about how soon after his wife had their baby, they were able to have sex again. Dr Guest used graphic language and spared no details. My patient at the time was a very nice woman in her fifties and she was obviously embarrassed by their rudeness. He talked as if we didn't even exist or as if we were so lowly that our existence was not even worth noticing. His arrogance was monumental. He had no right to be there teaching. He didn't know the first thing about instructing. All he knew was how to intimidate and abuse.

When I brought Dr Guest into my cubicle to approve my treatment plan, the first time I worked with him, he didn't say a word. He came in sat down, looked in Maria's mouth and left. He didn't say a word to Maria or myself. I didn't know what to do. Should I start the filling or not? Not wanting to begin without consent I went back to him to ask if it was okay to start. He was talking to another instructor at the time and when I walked up to him, Dr Guest deliberately and rudely turned his back on me. He continued talking to the other instructor. After about five minutes I finally tapped him on his bony shoulder and asked, "Dr Guest, is it alright if I start the filling now?" Dr Guest glanced at me as if I was a piece of dust on the end of a snotball. "What do you think?"was his response and he turned around to continue his discussion on the stock market.

Holy shit, I thought to myself. This guy is really an asshole. I walked back to my cubicle and started. After about fifteen minutes I had Maria anaesthetized and the rubber dam on. I was ready to start the filling. I popped my head up over the cubicle and looked around for Dr Guest. He was nowhere in sight. I figured it would be okay to start the prep. My other operative instructors had been pretty lenient with regards to the rubber dam by this time and subsequently they didn't worry about checking it off. I was working on Maria's tooth when about five minutes later I felt a sharp jab in the shoulder.

* * *

It was Dr Guest grinning like a Cheshire cat. At this point in time I didn't know that his grin meant that he was actually angry. "What do you think you're doing?" he demanded in his kindest ,cruel voice. Still not realizing my peril I kept my tone casual, "Oh, hello sir, I couldn't find you to check off the rubber darn so I started anyways. I hope that's okay with you." "You did what?" he demanded again. A lot less casual I replied, "I thought it would be okay to begin."

He continued grinning and beckoned for me to come with him by motioning with the index finger of his wizened hand. He walked to the outside of the cubicle and I followed. "Listen," he said sweetly, but with a definite undertone of malice. "Why is it that fifty-one others in your class have to get the rubber dam checked off, but not you? What makes you so special?"Each time he said "you, he poked me in the chest with his same index finger as if to physically drive home his point.

He was still grinning and it was obvious he was enjoying his own performance. Dr Guess had arranged it so my patient could clearly see my humiliation. He continued reaming me out in a slightly louder voice. "I'm going to have to fail you for today's performance since you haven't followed the proper clinical pro-tocol." I felt like shit. Maria had heard the entire conversation. I was afraid she might lose confidence in my abilities.

When I started back to work on Maria my hands were shak-ing. No matter how well I performed for the rest of the filling I was still getting a failing mark. It wasn't fair. I felt totally frus-trated. Trying to calm down I kept drilling. When I finished prep-ping the tooth I reluctantly called Dr Guest over again. He took a quick glance at the tooth and then looked at his Pearl Rolex, "I want to be out of here by quarter to five." With that announce-ment he walked out of my cubicle.

Again I wasn't sure what to do. Was it okay to continue or should I ask him to make sure. It was four o'clock. If he wanted to make me feel pressure he was doing a great job. I placed the protective base layer on the prep and then matrixed and wedged the tooth properly. I called Dr Guess over again. This time he sat down, took a quick look, shook his head in disgust and walked out. Now I really didn't know what to do. It was four fifteen and getting closer to four forty five by the second. I decided to continue. I mixed the amalgam and condensed the soft metal mass into the tooth. I had removed the wedges and matrix band and was carving the filling when I felt another jab in my shoulder "Here, let me finish," Dr Guest grinned. He butchered the filling with a couple quick scrapes of the carver and took the rubber dam off, all in about fifteen seconds. After checking the bite he dismissed my patient. It was now four forty three.

"Here," he said with obvious disdain and thrust a mark card into my hand. He gave me a U (Unsatisfactory) for rubber dam placement but S (Satisfactory) for everything else. I felt totally drained. I knew I would have a throbbing tension headache later on. What an asshole, I thought to myself.

The worst thing about Dr Guest was that he was unavoidable. Even if you were working with another instructor he would barge right in anyways and take over. Every single time I worked with him, he gave me a rough time. He always found some reason to mark me down. Eventually all I had to do was look at him and my stomach would knot up.

The timing for my one-week rotation in general medicine was superb. Poised right in the middle of second quarter it gave me a much needed break from the clinic. Not having to call patients and wheedle them to set up appointments was an added bonus. On the down side it was depressing knowing that you weren't getting any closer to finishing your clinical requirements.

Our rotation started with a Monday morning visit to a local hospital's Emergency Department. Besides myself, there was Steve, Barb and Marcia. Steve was probably the only true artsy in the class. He stood out because of his spiked hair and Matrix style apparel. Steve seldom if ever associated with anyone else from the class. He was determined to retain his sense of identity. So far he'd been doing fine. Marcia was a sweet girl with less than average looks and a lumpy dump body. Probably because she had no tits and ass to flaunt in front of the instructors she had to work just as hard as the rest of us.

I was glad Barb was in our group. She and I were still good friends and it was great having someone with you, whom you could relate to. I just wish we hadn't slept together in second year.

In the emergency room that morning we observed a diverse range of unremarkable illnesses and injuries. When an eighty-year-old woman was being examined for a suspected broken hip I almost passed out. Myself, Steve and the emergency room doctor were all crammed into a bathtub-sized examination room. It was stiflingly hot and when the doctor unwrapped her bath-robe and nightgown a sweet, cloying pungent odor inundated the room. She had a raised purple welt the size of a grapefruit on the upper lateral border of her iliac crest. As the doctor cautiously pressed his hands along the sides of the welt she cried out in a splashy, mewing sound. I saw a thick milky yellow white fluid ooze from her wound and simultaneously smelt a hot, rotting decay in the air. The walls of the room seemed to close in and I knew I had to leave. Steve followed less than a minute later. He whispered loudly in my ear, "Euu, did you smell that? Gross me out man!" Steve and I left the emergency room, sneaking out an hour early. We'd seen enough.

That afternoon we spent at a cancer clinic. First we listened to a short informative lecture on the treatment modalities and facilities for combating cancer and then we met real live cancer patients. Some were cured, some were being cured, some were dying. All the patients showed an eagerness to talk about their conditions. It was educational in a way that textbooks and lectures could never be. Particularly poignant was the sixty-year-old man whose face was only half there, talking in a hoarse, raspy whisper about his surgery and facial prosthesis, while simultaneously chain smoking his precious cigarettes. Oddly enough, all the patients we saw that afternoon were smokers. I reminded myself not to start the habit.

The next day was devoted to children. In the morning we went to a home for handicapped children and in the afternoon we toured the recently-opened facilities of the new children's hospital. At the home for handicapped kids I was a little preoccupied to enjoy the tour, after Barb filled me in on a secret. She had worked at the home the previous summer and during her tenure there she'd picked up a nasty infestation of scabies.

Scabies are particularly gruesome because they crawl and burrow right underneath your skin. All that day and even the next I was scratching and itching from head to toe.

The children's hospital was simply amazing. Everything was brand new and sparkling clean. All the faces of the staff from janitor to the most senior surgeon looked caring, eager and strong. They had a powerful conviction in their jobs that shone through in their faces, and I think I was a little jealous. Suddenly dentistry and teeth seemed pretty trivial, especially when compared to those who dealt with life and death on a daily basis.

On the third day of our rotation we observed surgical procedures. Steve and I arrived before the others. We were to observe a cleft lip and palate repair which had been scheduled for 9 am in operatory three of the surgical floor. It was eight thirty when Steve and I decided we might as well put on the necessary sterile garb so we could get in the operatory early. That way we'd be assured of a good seat. No one else was in the changing room when we put on the blue scrub pants,tops, masks and hats which were mandatory attire in the operating rooms.

When we walked into operatory three, there were five or six people milling about, getting things organized. As we stood there, not sure of where we should go, they all stopped what they were doing and just stared at us. I heard a few giggles and a suppressed laughing sound. Feeling stupid I said to nobody in particular, "We're the dental students." A shapely nurse finally said, "You better stand over there,"pointing to the far corner, "so you don't get in the way."

It was then that I realized no one was wearing the same kind of hats we were. In fact, feeling my face flush a hot red, I realized we were wearing booties on our heads, not hats! I started laughing and shaking under my mask. I tried to tell Steve but I was laughing too hard. I managed to eke out, "Our hats" and saw Steve wildly looking around. We both scurried out of the room at the same time, trying to blend in with the walls. As soon as we were out of the O.R. we burst out laughing. Talk about embarrassing. We went back to the change room and stripped off our operating room garb. We both decided it would be too humiliating to return to the O.R. so we went for breakfast in the hospital cafeteria instead. We never did see the cleft lip/cleft palate repair.

That afternoon we went to a different hospital to observe an oral surgeon extracting wisdom teeth. In the two hours we were there Dr Lee saw eight patients and extracted thirty teeth. I was totally awed by his skill and speed. The anesthetist was even having a hard time keeping up. No sooner would the anesthetist have the patient unconscious and stabilized, when Dr Lee would be sewing up the last suture. It was like an assembly line.

Roll the half-naked body into the room, put them to sleep with a needle, hook them up to a monitoring machine, intubate them, whip out the teeth, place a few sutures, take out the intubator, get them breathing on their own, roll them out and roll in the next patient. All of Dr Lee's motions were liquid, graceful and flowing. I never saw him having to push or pull or use any apparent force. He did it all by technique, yet it seemed more like magic. The teeth appeared to almost pop out on their own. When he put sutures in, his hands went so fast they blurred. There was no roughness, no bruising and no sweat.

One young woman that came rolling in was beautiful. As the anesthetist taped on his electrodes and wires I couldn't help but stare at her breasts. They were large and her nipples were erect. She seemed nothing more than a slab of meat and I felt a strong sexual desire. When Dr Lee cut with his scalpel and I saw the thin line of red, I looked back at her breasts and wanted to squeeze them roughly with my hands. Disgusted and excited at the same time I tried to analyze my feelings. I think it was the harsh, sterile environment which made me rebel and seek human values. The only human emotion I could isolate in that setting was lust. I think there was an element of voyeurism as well.

I'm sure the patient had no idea dental students would be watching her surgery, staring at her breasts. I wondered if I would ever see that patient again. Watching Dr Lee I also wondered if I'd ever develop the skill and dexterity that he had. I couldn't help but feel so inadequate, knowing the limited scope of my skills at that time.

The next day we had the morning off due to a scheduling screw up. In the afternoon we observed one of our profs at his private oral medicine clinic. During the three-hour clinic Dr Banda saw a patient roughly every ten minutes. Watching Dr Banda in action was fascinating. I wondered why the rest of dental school couldn't be as stimulating.

One patient had a small growth on the underside of his tongue. Dr Banda took a quick look and then explained to the patient that the growth should be removed and biopsied. He had the patient sign a consent form and then rammed a needle into the floor of the patient's mouth to freeze the area. Next he grabbed the tip of the tongue in cotton gauze and injected several more times right into the tongue. It looked painful but the patient barely flinched.

* * *

The biopsy itself took about two seconds. Dr Banda grabbed the growth with a pair of cotton pliers and made two small incisions with a scalpel at it's base, severing the growth from the tongue. That was it. Dr Banda plopped the growth into a biopsy bottle and then placed two sutures in the wound. The whole procedure from beginning to end took about five minutes.

The entire time Dr Banda worked he fired questions at us. Surprisingly with the four of us, there were very few questions we couldn't answer. I realized that although we had a long way to go, we were at least part-way there. We saw patients with trigeminal neuralgia (both typical and atypical),migraines, cluster headaches, lupus, Alzheimer's and even a rare glandular disorder, Sjogren's syndrome.

On Friday we ended our week with a visit to another hospital to watch yet another oral surgeon in action. The surgeon, Dr Prent, was one of our oral surgery professors and he was in his early sixties. It was rumored he had been offered early retirement to get him out of the operating room. I soon found out why. In contrast to Dr Lee from a few days earlier Dr Prent was brutal. In the morning he had only two patients yet it took him almost three hours to extract eight teeth in all.

Where Dr Lee was flowing and gentle in motion, Dr Prent was rough, unsure and jerky. His hands were shaking quite noticeably when he was suturing and the sutured wounds,instead of looking neat and tidy, looked more like Dr Frankenstein's work.

When Dr Prent placed a forceps or elevator on a tooth, you could see the muscles in his arm and shoulders bulging and the sweat forming on his forehead. While extracting the last tooth on his first patient he grabbed the patient's mandible so hard I noticed bruising afterwards when he took his hand away. I made a mental note to never let this guy near my mouth. I wondered how and why he was still practicing. And then I realized maybe he had always been a rotten surgeon and not just in the autumnal down slide of his career. Scary thought. But what can you expect from a guy who wore bright orange clogs in the operating room?

Despite his faults in the operating room, Dr Prent was an excellent and compassionate teacher, as I would soon discover during my oral surgery rotation.

That afternoon we were supposed to observe Dr Prent again, but his only patient cancelled. With the idea of escape in mind I caught the two o'clock train to visit my parents for the weekend. I spent a lot of the weekend at Sue's and my parents couldn't understand why I came home if I wasn't going to spend some time with them. How could I tell them that I spent most of the weekend having fun with Sue. In fact the weekend was so great I entertained the notion of staying there, never returning to dental school, forgetting about the clinic, maybe getting a job. But when Sunday night came, there I was on the train, heading back to school, the clinic and my patients.

My first rotation in the oral surgery clinic came only two weeks after general medicine. Again it was a welcome relief from the stress of the regular clinic. The patients we saw in oral surgery were booked by the secretaries in the department and all we had to do was show up. Regrettably we had no idea what clinical procedures we'd be performing. For our first rotation it didn't really matter because we'd mostly just be watching. The fourth year students assigned with us to the clinic would be doing the majority of extractions. Ninety-nine percent of what was done in the oral surgery clinic was extractions. Each week six third year and six fourth year students sweated it out with Nurse Watson.

Nurse Watson was a dental school tradition. She'd been in the oral surgery department since it's inception and she was the one who really ran the department. If you wanted to pass your oral surgery rotation you stayed on her good side. To achieve this all you had to do was 1- obey her every command and 2- know how much codeine was in a tylenol #1, #2, and #3. Nurse Watson can best be described as a Roseanne clone. She was a very large, loud, sarcastic, bitter woman. She'd sit behind her desk like an army commander, assigning us to patients according to her whims. There was always a can of diet coke or diet 7-up in front of her along with the day's copy of the Globe and Mail. Who was she trying to kid? For every diet coke she drank she probably wolfed down a chicken or two when she got home. As for the Globe and Mail, that was a joke too. She was a National Enquirer reader if I ever saw one.

But despite her faults, in the oral surgery clinic she was GOD. In her own way she was fair. She never appeared to play favorites and she treated the so-called hotshots of dentistry the same as everyone else. If anything Nurse Watson liked to give the hotshots a hard time and bring them down a notch.

Two of the most obnoxious assholes in our class were in our first rotation. Julio and Alex. Julio, a slimy Lebanese, seriously thought he was God's gift to both dentistry and women. Alex walked like he had a pickle up his ass, but never noticed because his nose was already way too high in the air. I instinctively disliked and avoided them both. For the entire oral surgery rotation they kept to themselves and hardly said a word to anyone else, except for our token female, Tracy. Tracy's father was a dentist who'd been past president of a powerful dental association. That was the only way I could figure out that she'd gotten into dental school. But I had no idea how she passed each year. It was rumored her father had conditionally donated a large sum of money to the faculty. The condition was that his daughter receive her degree in dentistry. Tracy reminded me of Veronica from the old Archies comic books.

Luckily Paul was also amongst our six. I didn't know any of the fourth year students except for Gord and that was by reputation only. Supposedly Gord was one of two fourth year students who were totally spastic. Each year the faculty tried to expel Gord and his classmate Lester for gross incompetence but every year Gord and Lester got their lawyers on their case and every year the dynamic duo won. Lester was supposedly both a moron and a spazz while Gord was rumored to just be a spazz. Our first morning in oral surgery was an orientation session for third year students while the fourth year students got started with the patients. Nurse Watson talked to us about procedure, paperwork and sterile technique. By the time she was finished I was almost asleep. As far as the important procedures were concerned we were to follow the same routine with every patient. 1- Take the patient's medical history, blood pressure, temperature, heart rate and respiration rate. 2-Diagnose the problem and formulate a treatment plan. 3-Present the diagnosis and treatment plan to an instructor and 4-Carry out the treatment plan.

The instructors in the oral surgery department were either staff on the faculty of dentistry or oral surgeons in private practice who sacrificed an afternoon or morning of their time to teach.

After Nurse Watson's talk we dispersed to the individual operatories to watch the fourth year students. Hoping to see some action I went to Gord's room. Unfortunately I couldn't see very much since the room was crowded and I was the last person in. Every time the fourth year student (not Gord) put his forceps on the patient's tooth, the patient started moaning. And then whenever the patient moaned, the student stopped and asked the patient if it hurt. The patient said no it was fine, and then the student put his forceps back on the tooth and the process repeated itself again and again.

Eventually the instructor Dr Prent came to the rescue. Without fanfare Dr Prent grabbed the tooth with the forceps, eliciting a surprised yelp from the patient in response. Without pausing Dr Prent proceeded to lift the patient's tooth and whole head off the chair. The patient screamed, the tooth popped out like a watermelon seed between two fingers and the patient's head flopped back down on the chair. Although not very pretty, the quick and dirty technique was at least effective.

That afternoon Nurse Watson assigned me my first oral surgery patient. She'd already assigned almost everyone else. There were only three of us left and I remember thinking I was safe. No such luck. She looked me square in the eyes and barked, "Ken, take care of the patient in operatory two and bring Paul with you to assist."

My patient Mary was twelve years old and so frightened that when we walked into the room she started crying. I introduced myself and Paul and we took her vital signs and medical history. She'd been sent from the orthodontics department to have a retained deciduous molar extracted. The x-ray of the tooth showed roots that looked like pincers. There appeared to be no resorption of the primary molar's roots. It wouldn't be an easy extraction.

We tried to calm Mary down but she was so afraid, our efforts had little effect. When we brought Dr Prent in so we could present our case she started wailing. I wondered if they had met before. Dr Prent listened patiently to our presentation, nodding his head occasionally. When we finished he took us outside the room, being sure to close the door behind us. He basically told us that the kid seemed like a little bugger. He recommended that we use nitrous oxide (laughing gas) to calm her down, and he wanted us to keep the door closed so the sounds wouldn't disrupt the rest of the clinic. If the tooth wasn't out by four o'clock we were to call him in.

With his words of wisdom we went back to give Mary the good news. She was getting laughing gas. She didn't sound too thrilled and when we strapped on the nitrous mask she started crying again. We tried to reassure her as best as we could but she kept on crying. As we turned the gas on I noticed no change in her sobbing. After a couple of minutes she finally stopped crying and after five minutes I could see her eyelids start to droop.

We had her open her mouth and Paul gave her the injection of local anesthetic. When she felt the pinprick of the needle going in she screamed bloody murder. I couldn't believe a twelve-year-old girl was capable of screaming so loud.

After the injection I patted her shoulder and told her the worst part was over. Nothing would hurt anymore. We turned up the gas higher and waited for the freezing to take. Paul and I shot the shit, while our patient calmed down, and almost fell asleep. Fifteen minutes passed and we decided to start. Mary was by now quite relaxed and we asked her to open her mouth. I tested the anesthetic by jabbing a sharp explorer into her gums adjacent to the tooth I was going to be extracting. There was no reaction from her so I knew she was frozen. Next I told Mary I would be grabbing on to her tooth and wiggling it back and forth until it came out. She seemed agreeable. When she saw the shiny steel forceps in my hand I could see she wasn't quite so sure. As soon as I touched the forceps against her tooth she started crying. I stopped, took the forceps off her tooth and asked her what was wrong. She said it hurt. I told her it couldn't hurt because her tooth was asleep. She countered by saying it wasn't the tooth that was hurting, but her gums. I humored her and took the sharp explorer out again. I had her open her mouth and again I pushed the sharp point into her gums, first very gently and then harder. No response. She was obviously frozen. I told her as much and I even admitted I'd just jabbed her gum with a sharp point. "Ouch!" she said.

I asked her if I could try to wiggle her tooth again. She hesitantly agreed and let me put the forceps on the tooth. No problem. As soon as I applied pressure she started crying again. By this time I'd had enough of her. I just kept on applying pressure and wiggling the tooth a little to the left, then a little to the right, just like we'd been taught. After a few minutes of having her tooth wiggled she realized it wasn't hurting and finally stopped crying. My hand felt like it was ready to cramp up. I let Paul work at it for a few minutes to give myself a rest.

Neither of us made much head-way until I tried again. Suddenly it started wiggling more to the right and left each time and then the tooth came right out. The roots were incredibly thin and fragile looking but they were intact. I couldn't believe I hadn't broken a root tip. Mary was so happy to have the tooth finally come out, she started crying again. We had Mary bite down on a rolled-up piece of cotton gauze and we called Dr Prent over. I showed him the tooth, long spindly roots and all. He gave Paul and myself marks of eighty-five percent for in his words, managing a difficult patient.

The next day passed relatively uneventfully. I'd proven myself with Nurse Watson the day before, so some of the pressure was off. In the morning Paul and I watched Gord take out an upper wisdom tooth. The patient, a low-life, long-haired, stinky guy in his twenties didn't look too thrilled to be there. He kept on asking Gord if he'd ever taken a tooth out before. Maybe the patient had heard the rumors about him.

As was the custom, a third year student, myself, administered the local anesthetic. When the patient learned he was getting a needle he turned a sickly shade of white with big beads of sweat popping out on his forehead. Looking at the ornate tattoo of an eagle on the patient's forearm I suggested he pretend he was getting a tattoo in his mouth. He responded to my grim humor by coughing up a big phlegm ball that he spit into the adjacent sink.

This was something I encountered frequently as a dental student. Big tough guys with tattoos all over themselves, turning white and almost fainting at the prospect of getting one single needle in the mouth. As I brought the needle up to the patient's mouth he closed his eyes tightly while his whole body shook. Altogether it took three separate needles to freeze the area. I injected the first and Paul did the last two.

We were ready to see Gord in action and we had front row seats. Imagine our surprise when

Gord smoothly and very confidently finessed the tooth out in all of ten seconds. As Gord showed the freshly extracted tooth to the very relieved patient, Paul and I looked at each other. We were both thinking the same thing. Did we just witness what actually happened? Gord was supposed to be one of the two worst students in fourth year and yet his extraction had looked more like a skilled oral surgeons' than a struggling dental student.

After Gord gave the patient post-op instructions, the patient shook all our gloved hands, thanked us profusely and briskly headed out of the clinic. Probably to the nearest open tavern.

As we were all removing our latex gloves and washing I said to Gord, "Wow, you made that look easy." My praise was genuine and his face lit up at the compliment.

Gord told us how he'd spent most of his summer working at an oral surgery clinic in Israel. Apparently it was like taking a graduate course in oral surgery and he'd been taught a lot of good techniques. Techniques that Paul and I wouldn't have learned if it wasn't for Gord. I thought to myself- if they could take one of the worst students and turn him into a competent tooth puller, then there was hope for me.

During the rest of the week we watched Gord in action as much as we could. We learned more from him than from all our oral surgery lectures and professors combined. He showed both Paul and I how to use an elevator properly. An elevator is a surgical tool that looks like a screwdriver. The tip is placed between teeth and by rotating the elevator you can actually move teeth enough to loosen them from their bony sockets.

Additionally Gord showed us how to use a forceps properly. Instead of grabbing a tooth and pulling, the right technique is to push down with the forceps to make the tooth pop out like a watermelon seed between two fingers. Gord even warned us which instructors to avoid in operative dentistry and fixed prosthodontics. It was the first time I'd ever really bonded with an upper year classmate.

* * *

I'm sure if any instructors noticed Gord coaching us they assumed it was a case of the blind leading the blind. They couldn't be further from the truth. I was learning that the best education often came from unexpected sources.

On Wednesday afternoon Paul,Gord and myself saw a twenty-two-year-old psychology student who was complaining of a sore jaw. She had an extra tooth erupting between her first molar and premolar on her lower right. Only the tip of the erupting tooth could be seen,but all around the area it was red and very swollen. The patient was an anomaly in the clinic because not only was she very attractive, she was also very nice and she definitely was not a lowlife.

We all kind of pranced around like we were real hotshots but she easily saw through our bravado. "So what are you, second or third year students?" she asked. Feeling a little deflated I admitted that Paul and I were third year students while Gord was in his fourth year. "So you guys are taking out my tooth?" she asked hesitantly while raising her eyebrows and looking right at Gord. We said that we didn't know yet.

When Dr Prent came in the room, he took one glance at the x-ray, the patient and then us. Dr Prent said he himself would do the extraction. Her case was supposedly an ideal case to use as a teaching demonstration. He arranged for her to return to the clinic the next morning at nine o'clock.

After she left Dr Prent told us the real reason he would be extracting the tooth. Apparently the root of the tooth was sitting directly on top of the nerve that supplied all the sensory and motor sensation to the right lower jaw. There was a possibility of damaging this nerve while extracting the tooth.

Just the week before a similar nerve had been nicked inadvertently by a third year student and the patient still had a partial paralysis in the jaw. The ultimate legal responsibility was with the instructor who was supervising at the time. Dr Prent did not want a similar occurrence.

Weeks later, through a lot of snooping and prying I finally found out who the student was who nicked the nerve. I was shocked since I'd always thought of him as being very competent. Due to the patient's unusual anatomy it wasn't his fault. Despite the absolution of blame it still hung like a black cloud over the student for the next two years since the patient remained partially paralyzed.

When incidents of this magnitude occurred they were kept very hush-hush. It was only through a lot of persistent questioning and even some obnoxious prying that I discovered the facts in the partial paralysis case. This was the only case I heard of in my entire time at dental school where any patient suffered any form of permanent damage. In reality it was probably safer to go to our dental school to have work done than it was to see any dentist in private practice. In dental school you were always assured of having close, expert supervision. Despite this high quality of care there were a couple other incidents in third year where patients sustained some temporary damage.

One event happened in the regular dental clinic. A student was drilling away at a patient's tooth when his hand slipped and he ended up drilling an inch long gash through the floor of his hapless patient's mouth. The patient needed four stitches to close the wound. To make matters worse, the patient had been a dental assistant. I laughed when I heard the news. Not because I'm sadistic and think it's funny when people get hurt but because the student who screwed up was no other than

Rob Lerner, the most arrogant of all the arrogant assholes in my class. It was refreshing to see his ego bruised.

The other incident occurred in SPEC. Barb had done a routine filling on an upper tooth on a five-year-old. Unintentionally she had injected local anesthetic into a sinus space and later that night the child had to be hospitalized. Both of these patients recovered rapidly from their mishaps. The frail ego of a dental student was much harder to recover. Barb took the incident very personally. She thought that she had almost killed her patient and she felt totally responsible for the mishap. No amount of reassurance would sway her opinion. Her guilt grew like a tumor, sapping her confidence and ability. Eventually one of our SPEC instructors, in a rare moment of humanity, reassured Barb that it wasn't her fault and that it could have happened to anyone. I would question his motives because they started dating soon after the mishap. Regardless Barb was still deeply affected by the event and for the next two years she seemed to be in a constant state of depression. I wasn't surprised to learn in fourth year that Barb was taking antidepressants. Probably a third of our class was on some form of anti-stress medication by this time.

Dr Prent removed Iva's tooth uneventfully while all twelve of us students watched. He removed the tooth rather swiftly with the aid of a chisel and mallet. Although the procedure looked quite barbaric Iva felt no pain and suffered no resultant nerve damage. I was particularly grateful Dr Prent hadn't damaged the nerve for purely personal reasons.

A week later, by pure coincidence, I met Iva at a bar downtown. She recognized me right away and we started chatting. One thing led to another and eventually we ended up on the couch in my apartment with her lips stuck to mine. It was quite obvious there was nothing wrong with her motor or sensory nerve innervation. Iva and I had a lot of fun that evening.

I tried calling her to set up a date after but she was always busy. Eventually I got the hint and stopped calling. As far as I was concerned meeting Iva was a fringe benefit of being a dental student. Of course I wouldn't/couldn't get involved with any of the regular clinic patients. That seemed totally unethical. With Iva I knew she didn't have any dental work that still needed to be done, and subsequently I would never see her in the clinic again.

Some students in our class ended up going out with their regular patients. To me this seemed just too weird. Maybe I was jealous because the opportunity never came up for me. One student in our class married a woman he first met as one of his patients. Ironically the marriage only lasted three months.

The rest of the week in oral surgery passed uneventfully. Except for getting our hepatitis B booster shots. Nurse Watson insisted on delivering the booster personally. And she only believed in administering the booster in the gluteus maximus muscle. So she had all of us line up and pull our pants down. She loved it. She even had the nerve to award a prize to the best ass each week. I was disappointed and relieved that I didn't win. Those honors went to Paul and we never let him forget it. Poor sucker. I found out later that Nurse Watson had pulled a fast one on us. The booster was most effective if delivered in the arm. She just wanted to see all of our bare bums. Man was she sick.

The next week I returned to the main clinic. It was almost Christmas. Time to take stock of my progress. I was gaining speed and confidence but unfortunately not making much progress with my clinical requirements, especially in operative dentistry. So far I'd finished twelve surfaces of silver fillings out of a required seventy-five, five out of eighteen white fillings, and hadn't started the gold inlays or done either of my practical exams. I was worried. It's not that I was screwing up. On the contrary my marks had been quite good. It was just that half the year was over and I still had three quarters of the assigned requirements to get through.

As far as my other clinical courses were concerned I was doing fine. In endodontics I'd finished five root canals, and in orthodontics and periodontics I'd accumulated more that an average number of points. In removable prosthodontics I was almost finished Dorothy's denture.

Skit night for third year was depressing. We really wanted to shit on our instructors but we didn't dare. We still had too much school ahead of us to piss them off. We ended up doing a fairly restrained version of Dental Family Feud.

We had Dr Moore, Dr Willis and Dr Yank on the Restorative Team and Dr Imanka, Dr Thomsky and Dr Edmund on the Preventative Team. Our host of the game was our class president, Tom Johnson. He started out, "Welcome to our down and dirty version of Dental Family Feud. Tonight we have two teams, The Restorative Team and The Preventative team. For the Restorative team we have Dr Mini- Moore, Dr Wise-ass- Willis and Dr Yuck-yank. Their opponents for tonight are the totally clueless Preventative Team consisting of Dr Immense-Imanka, Dr Terrible Thomsky and Dr Ex -lax- Edmund.

Why don't we start off with our first question. Remember a hundred people were surveyed and top five answers are on the board. Dr Moore and Dr Imanka, are you ready? Name a car that starts with Pee? Yes, Dr Moore. " "I' m sorry but I don't believe any car starts with pee, they all start with gas."

"Alrighty then, the answer for the Restorative Team is, none! I'm sorry that is not one of the top five answers.Dr Imanka, it's your turn." " Ah Porsche" "Yes Dr Imanka, that is the number two answer, with twenty-eight percent. Number one answer was Pontiac with fifty-three percent. Preventative Team do you wish to play or pass?" "We'll play,"responded the preventative team." "Okay next question is, How many dental students does it take to change a light bulb? Dr Thomsky? " "Yes, I think the answer is five. One to hold the bulb and four to turn the ladder." "Well, let's see if five is up there? Ah, yes it is number five on the list, with eight percent. Preventative Team, you go again. Dr Edtnund what is your answer? " " I don't think that students are afraid of the dark, so my answer is none. Do you understand?" "Okay then, let's check the board and see if none is one of the top five answers. I'm sorry, none is not one of the top five answers.

Restorative Team this is your chance to pull ahead. What is your answer?" After a quick huddle with his peers Dr Moore responds, "We think the answer is two.One to mix the martinis and one to call the electrician." "Alright let's check our board. Two is the number two answer with twenty -five percent. Number one answer was one with fifty-one percent. Oh and by the way, two is the number one answer for how many dental professors it takes to change a light bulb. Okay next question, what is something that a blind man uses? Dr Willis what is your answer?" "Well, I'll have to say a sword." Dr Willis's team-mates are congratulating him, "Good answer, good answer!" " I'm sorry, team restorative, but that is not one of the top five answers. Team preventative, what is your answer? Dr Imanka?" "That's a tough one, but I'll have to say a flashlight." "I'm sorry Dr Irnanka that is not one of our top five answers. Next question, who has the highest IQ from the following list. A- Dental Professors, B-Dental Students, C-Gym Teachers, D-Bill Gates, E-Pond Scum, F-Lawyers, G-Morons or H-Actuaries. We have the top three answers on our board.. Restorative Team, you're up. Dr Yank?" "This is a ridiculously easy answer. I'm going to say dental professors, of course." " I'm sorry Dr Yank that answer is not one of the top three. It's back to you now Preventative Team. Yes, Dr

Moore, what is your answer?" "I'm going to say pond scum." "Good choice, that is the number three answer with twenty-one percent of the vote. Number one answer here was B-Dental students with sixty-five percent. Restorative Team you have successfully defeated the preventative team. Who is representing your team for the final round? Yes Dr Edmund. You will have twenty seconds to answer the four questions. If you can't think of an answer you can pass. Are you ready, Dr Edmund? Name a popular ladies' fashion item. Start the clock" " Ah, I'll have to pass." "Name something people clean their hair with."

"Ah I'll have to pass again." "What is a common phrase meaning, are you aware of what you're doing?" Yes Alex, that would be - Do you understand?" " Name something people put under their armpits to stop body odor."

"Ah, ... pass."

"Time is up. Okay Dr Edmunds, let's check your answers and see how you've done. The only question you answered was number three and you said, "Do you understand?" That was the number one answer with sixty-seven percent. Very Good."

"Now, Restorative Team, you must get one hundred and thirty three points if you want to win the grand prize for today. This time you will have thirty seconds on the clock, if you hear a special buzzer, your answer is the same as Dr Edmunds and you must try again. Who have you chosen for your final round? Ah Dr Imanka, are you ready? Name a popular woman's fashion item? Start the clock." " Uhh, Meenie skirt." "Name something people clean their hair with," Shumpoo." "What is a common phrase meaning, are you aware of what you're doing?" "Toyo koto si osakee?" "Name something people put under their armpits to stop body odor." "Dee-oh-dah-lint."

"Alright let's check your answers Dr Imanka. A popular ladies' fashion item. You said a meenie-skirt. Miniskirt was the number one answer with fifty-one percent of the vote. Something people clean their hair with. You said, shumpoo. Again shampoo was the number one answer with fifty-five percent of the vote. What is a common phrase meaning, are you aware of what you're doing? You said, Toyo koto si osakee. I'm sorry that is not one of our top five answers. Our last question was, Name something people put under their armpits to stop body odor. You said, Dee-oh-dah-lint. You need twenty-eight percent to win, I'm sorry but dee-oh da-lint was not in the top five answers. Number one answer was deodorant with sixty percent of the vote. I'd like to thank both teams tonight for their extraordinary efforts. And to everyone I wish a good night.

The response from the audience was only lukewarm. Once again the fourth year class had the best skit. They did a spoof of Let's Make a Deal that was truly hilarious.

Our set of exams before Christmas were relatively easy compared to the first two years. They were mostly short-answer, paragraph-style questions. And the questions were right from our notes. There were no surprises. When I finished the last exam I was ecstatic. I hopped on a train right after and went home for the holidays. My parents were glad to see me so happy. That night I went out drinking with them. My dad got really drunk and became very emotional. It was totally unlike his normal self. He was brought up in the Finnish, Nordic fashion. You never asked for help and were totally self-sufficient. Most of all you never showed your emotions no matter what. That night he started crying that our family would never be the same again, that he didn't love my mother and never had, that his life was totally unfulfilled and that he needed to be on his own to discover himself. My whole world was rocked. I couldn't believe that I was part of a broken family. That night I couldn't sleep. My father's truths had struck me right in the heart and I felt partially responsible.

The next day my father was up early. I asked him how he was feeling. He said that he was fine. He had forgotten everything he had said the night before and pretended that everything was normal. I never heard him ever complain about his life again. And they stayed married. It was like the whole night before had never happened. And we never talked about it. That was taboo. I spent a little time with Sue over the holidays but she had a new boyfriend and wasn't interested in getting physical with me anymore. I tried to get together with Kareena but she was now working in Ottawa and we had to call it quits because of the distance. Anne was still interested in me but I had lost interest in her. All she wanted to do was talk about her old boy-friend. I just stopped calling her and didn't return her calls. By Christmas it was definitely over. She hadn't called me for three weeks. I called her to wish her a Merry Christmas but just got her answering machine. She never called me back. I spent most of my holiday sleeping in and watching old movies. The time went very quickly and before I knew it , it was time to go back.

In my first week back after the Christmas break Dr Imanka called me into his office for a little talk. He got right to the point. I was last in the class as far as number of clinical requirements completed. He wanted to know if I was having any problems. I told him no, I'd just gotten off to a slow start. Of course I didn't realize until then, that I was the slowest in the whole class. Dr Imanka emphasized that there would be no supplementals in third year operative dentistry. In other words if I didn't finish my operative clinical requirements by the end of the year I was in trouble. I would fail the year. Dr Imanka was very nice and extremely polite the whole time.

Before I left I told him he didn't have to worry. I would get my clinical requirements done. Later that week I did my first operative practical exam to prove my intent. The practical exam went very smoothly. I had picked Dr Imanka to mark me and he was very encouraging during the entire procedure. It was our one pin, practical exam and to pass we had to complete a silver filling with at least three surfaces and one steel pin placed prop-erly in the prep. The pin was difficult to place. I had to drill the hole for the pin first and then manually screw the small steel pin into the tooth. By the time I had screwed the pin in, I was sweat-ing. I had a moment of panic when Dr Imanka was checking the pin and I thought I saw him move the pin. It was supposed to be solidly embedded in the tooth and not mobile at all.

✳ ✳ ✳

Dr Imanka didn't say anything about the pin and I finished the rest of the filling with no problems. Dr Imanka gave me three G's (Goods) for the exam and I was thrilled.

Meanwhile I was wishing I was in a relationship again. I was lonely without female companionship. In February I got involved again. Actually I'd met Nancy earlier in the year at a pub in October but didn't ask her out because of my situation at the time. Nancy was a third year nursing student. I was attracted to her from the very first time I saw her. She was five feet two inches tall and had a wonderfully curvaceous shape that even her bulky sweaters couldn't conceal. Her eyes were dark, dark brown and every time I talked with her I noticed her pupils were enormous. I kept running into her at the cafeteria and library. When I saw her I always made a point to talk with her. That was how I learned her last name and that she was unattached.

In the last week of January I got my nerve up and asked her out. Since I knew her last name I called directory assistance and got her number. I still remember how nervous I was when I called her on a Wednesday evening. I felt like I was back in high school again. After some preliminary small talk I asked if she wanted to go out for drinks and dinner on Saturday night. In the background I heard one of my favorite songs by the Smiths. She said no. She had to study that night. I was devastated. But then she suggested Friday night instead. Happily I agreed and we arranged a time and a place to meet. And so Friday night ,February the first, I had my first date with Nancy, my future wife.

We went to Elephant and Castle. I had a burger and she had nachos. We each had a couple drinks and we had a magical evening. Afterwards she came back to my apartment and we kept talking. It was almost three in the morning when we realized how late it was. She decided to spend the evening and I was a perfect gentleman. I held her all night long. She was only wearing one of my oversize t-shirts and I could feel her wonderful curves right through her shirt, but I didn't dare anything overtly sexual. She was a beautiful, intelligent, fascinating woman and I wanted to take my time to get to know her. After that first night we were inseparable. We spent almost every night together either at my apartment or hers. It was wonderful to be in love and it made life in the clinic seem more bearable.

Undoubtedly my strangest patient in third year was Mary. She lived over a hundred miles from the clinic but came anyway because she needed crowns which she couldn't afford otherwise. Mary loved to talk. In each appointment from the minute I met her in the waiting room until I said my last good byes, she talked non-stop. It didn't matter that I had both hands in her mouth or that an impression tray was setting up in her mouth. She just wouldn't stop talking.

Mary had two boys, age four and seven, and a husband who alternatively either ignored or berated her. Despite having a university degree in English she was now a full-time housewife. Jokingly she referred to her status as domestic goddess. Mary really was a very smart lady. Her problem was that she was stuck at home all day with a kid and the soaps. Apparently her husband didn't approve of her having girlfriends and he also didn't like her going places on her own. Sadly, coming to the clinic was her one social outlet. She'd try to fit a whole week of talking into a three-hour appointment.

Her conversations ranged from the dwindling rain forests to democracy versus socialism to the horrible plight of third world refugees to even sex in marriage. No topic was taboo to Mary. Her younger boy was affected with a severe physical and mental handicap which kept him confined to a wheelchair. It was both difficult and costly for Mary to get a babysitter so she brought him along to her appointments. She'd wheel him into the cubicle, talking up a storm as usual and park him in the corner, promptly ignoring him for the next three hours. He was quiet and well-behaved until he heard the sound of the dental drill. He'd coo and drool happily and then the second I started the drill he went ape shit, screaming and crying. When I stopped drilling he stopped crying.

And so I prepared my first ever crown, listening to Mary's innate and senseless rambling, along with the background screams of the kid from hell. I wanted to take my needle and ram it into the top of the brat's head and then do the same for his mother.

After three hours of working on Mary's crown I was a mess. I had a splitting headache and my nerves were shot. I felt like

I'd depleted all my natural stores of adrenaline and serotonin. To make matters worse, right after Mary and her son left, I was called into the clinic administrator's office.

Apparently her son's screaming had been very disruptive to the clinic. The administrator had complaints from students, instructors and even a secretary who worked far down the hall from the clinic. She was sympathetic but firm. Mary's son was officially banned from the clinic.

When I phoned Mary to tell her, she was practically in tears. The next day her husband phoned me up to complain. He raved on and on about how much it was costing to have Mary come to the clinic. Especially now since they'd have to shell out twenty dollars each appointment for a babysitter. The gas was already costing over thirty dollars a visit. She drove an old clunker that got only slightly better gas mileage than a tank. How many more appointments would Mary need, he demanded to know.

I patiently explained to him that every-thing took longer to do at the clinic because all procedures needed to be closely supervised. I also reminded him that Mary's crown would only cost a hundred dollars at the clinic compared to five hundred dollars at a private practice. When I explained it to him in terms of money he calmed down, but not before he made a vague threat. He expected that her crown would be finished in three or four appointments at the very most. In fact it took five more appointments to finish Mary's crown. It took that long because I had to make the crown myself. First of all I had to take an accurate impression of her crown prep. The crown prep took two appointments to finish. Then I had to wax up the crown on top of the lab model of her crown. Next I had to embed the wax in a clay mold and pour hot molten gold into the clay mold. I was left with a perfect gold replica of the wax-up I had made. Finally I had to polish the crown until it was gleaming.

The very last step was to confirm an accurate fit in Mary's mouth and cement the gold crown with special glue. Mary at last was happy and so was I. All of my further crown and bridge cases would be made by a commercial dental laboratory so I wouldn't have to do half the work.

Mary had the weirdest excuses for cancelling appointments. One morning in early February she called me at six in the morning. Her appointment was for nine. What was her reasoning for cancelling? She'd looked out of her bedroom window and saw the smoke going straight up and out of the smokestacks and chimneys. It was just too cold she said. At that time I was glad she wanted to cancel. It meant I could sleep in, so I didn't argue. I looked out my bedroom window and saw the smoke coming out of chimneys. It was rising straight up. No wind at all. It did look bitterly cold. Later I thought about what she said and it didn't make any sense, but for some reason at six in the morning it did.

The emergency clinic was better known as the loony tune clinic. This unofficial but popularized name was due to two separate factorrs, the patients, and Dr Schwartz, the director of the clinic. Each by itself would be sufficient to make the atmosphere a little crazy but the two in combination had a most definite synergistic effect. Dr Schwartz was only a year or two from retirement and probably should have retired a decade before. Like so many of the other older instructors he was tall, gangly and almost completely bald. He always wore his white lab coat and Cary Grant style horn rimmed glasses. Dr Schwartz was not a good-looking man. Not then. Not ever. His face resembled the drabness of an Idaho potato. He needed to clip his nose hairs. In fact his nose hairs were the first thing I noticed about him. That and his horrendously foul breath.

He had the annoying habit of never finishing his sentences. Right in the middle of giving instructions to a student he'd stop, stare into space pensively for a few seconds, then shuffle away. I don't think he was aware that he'd left off in mid-sentence. He was actually hard of hearing. When you talked to him you had to turn the volume up a notch and speak very clearly. His voice was as gruff and raspy as crushed gravel so it was often difficult to understand him.

The only thing that Dr Schwartz really cared about was paperwork. Every thing had to be done in triplicate. He had a separate form for every procedure and a separate protocol for every form. A patient could be dead in the chair and he wouldn't give a shit as long as all the paperwork was filled out properly. If your paperwork was botched or incomplete you were in big trouble. He'd give you the old lecture on the importance of paperwork citing the fall of the Roman Empire as proof.

Fortunately Dr Schwartz never failed any students in the emergency clinic no matter how poorly they performed. It was generally known that his bark was worse than his bite

The patients that came to the emergency clinic were mostly losers. No one was ever turned away from Dr Schwartz's emergency clinic, no matter how virulent or contagious their disorder was or dangerous or despicable the patient was.

We got whacked-out drug addicts trying to get another fix of narcotic painkillers, pregnant ladies with herpes, low-life scum with toothaches who wouldn't go to a regular dentist because they couldn't afford it, and lonely, little old ladies with vague symptoms and nothing better to do.

During the emergency clinic rotation you never knew who or what you'd get next. My first week in the emergency clinic was in late February. As still relatively inexperienced clinicians we were only assigned one week of the clinic in third year. We'd have to endure two weeks in fourth year.

Once again the rotation was a welcome relief from having to phone patients for appointments but unfortunately it wasn't getting me any closer to finishing my clinical requirements. The emergency clinic was on the opposite side of the waiting room from the main clinic.

As I walked through the emergency clinic doors on that Monday morning in February I felt very unsure of myself.So Far I hadn't seen any dental emergencies. All the dentistry I'd done was pre-planned and I hadn't seen a patient with a real toothache yet. I wasn't sure if I'd know what to do. I didn't have to wait long to find out. My very first patient that morning had a massive toothache. Upon examining his mouth it was easy to see why. He had a lower molar that looked like a bomb had been dropped right in the center of it. Instead of a nice,healthy tooth there was a black hole with jagged edges of enamel sticking up around the perimeter of what had once been a tooth. The whole side of his face on that side was puffy and swollen. It was an obvious case of gross dental caries and gross dental neglect.

"Gee, you got to help me, doc," the patient pleaded. " My tooth broke a while back and a couple days ago it started to ache real bad. Now it's driving me nuts. I couldn't even sleep last night." Feeling a little honored by being called doc I politely asked, "When did you first notice that the tooth was broken?" Thinking for a while he finally responded proudly as if his answer was a great revelation. "Two or three years ago I think."

He was wearing dirty blue jeans ripped at the knees and a black AC/DC t-shirt. His general appearance was pretty scruffy and I certainly would not want to meet him in a dark alley. "Doc, you got to help me. The pain is killing me,"he begged, and this time he held the bottom of his jaw while slightly rocking his head back and forth.

I didn't know what to do. Obviously he was in a great deal of pain and it looked like the tooth was a goner. I filled all my forms in triplicate and got Dr Schwartz to have a look. Dr Schwartz didn't like to get his hands wet so he had me put the mouth mirror in the patient's mouth. While he looked his only comments were a barely audible, "Hmmmm" and then a slightly louder, "Ahsaa!"

He motioned for me to take the mirror out of the patient's mouth and then gestured again for me to follow him. We walked out of the room and down the hall. Putting his arm around me in a fatherly fashion Dr Schwartz gave me the scoop. "Let's write him a prescription for antibiotics and send him on his way. Obviously he doesn't take care of his teeth and there's no point in trying to save them. Let's send him on his way tout de suite ! And make sure you've filled out all your forms for me to sign." Dr Schwartz gave me a conspiratorial wink and hobbled away, down the hall.

When I told the patient we were giving him a prescription to take away the infection, he sounded relieved. After all the paperwork was finished and the patient walked out of the clinic with his precious prescription I finally felt relieved too.

Before my next patient I sat around and shot the shit with Allan, the other third year student in the emergency clinic for that week. We'd been through almost three years of dental school in the same class and I didn't really know him. We always said Hi to each other and sometimes even sat together in the cafeteria if our other friends weren't there. We were more than acquaintances and less than friends. We discovered we were both born in the same city up north. We were only three months apart in age. Other-wise we had nothing in common and no real reason to like each other. He loved dental school and couldn't understand why any one wouldn't love it. I didn't bother trying to explain. The rest of the week went very quickly and next thing I knew I was back to the regular clinic.

Three weeks before the March break I noticed a note for me on the clinic message board. Dr Thomsky, chairman of the fixed prosthodontics department, wanted to see me. My first reaction was to panic. Normally profs didn't concern themselves with students unless there was a problem. I decided to see Dr Thomsky right away and get it over with.

As I knocked on Dr Thomsky's door I thought it didn't make any sense. I had already finished my fixed clinical requirements for third year. I'd even got good marks for making Mary's crown. Besides I got along quite well with Dr Thomsky ever since I'd told him the joke about Yoko Ono in second year. He always went out of his way to say, Hi to me. I even had more respect for Dr T. than I had for most of our instructors, not because he liked me,(although that helped) but primarily because he was an intellectual. He had been one of the pioneer researchers in the field of gnathology. His name was footnoted in all of our dental occlusion textbooks, which was a hell of a lot more than most of our instructors had achieved.

Dr T. drove a black Audi and parked right in front of the dental sciences building. The only other person who could park there without getting towed was the dean of dentistry. Dr T may have had a touch of arrogance but in his case I think it was warranted.

After a few seconds of knocking Dr T opened his door and looked at me with a blank stare.

"Hi, I just got your note. You wanted to see me?" I asked wondering if he even remembered who

I was. Then as if a switch had been flicked on, inside his head Dr T's jade green eyes softened and he said. " I wanted to ask if you could do me a favor." I thought to myself, you name it. I'll jump through a loop, take the Audi down to the corner store and buy you a couple copies of Swank, whatever. Trying to look suitably enthusiastic I answered, "Sure." Dr T said, " Well Ken, we need some-one to help with our refresher course in contemporary dentistry during the March break. The course is for foreign dentists trying to get their license to practice dentistry in Canada. We always hire a student to insure that things run smoothly. If you're interested you'd act as a liaison between the foreign dentists and our teaching staff. And we'll pay you five-hundred dollars for the week. What do you think? Are you interested?" When he mentioned the money his right hand reached up to scratch his bald head in a sort of nervous twitch. It was an easy decision. I couldn't afford to go any where for the March break, so why not stay and at least make some money.

I said, "Sure I'd love to help. When does the course start?" Dr T looked relieved. " Good," he replied. "The course starts Saturday morning at 9 am and goes until the following Sunday evening. I'd like you to meet me in front of the main clinic at eight thirty Saturday morning."

After I left Dr T's office I reconsidered my decision. I realized I would be at the dreaded clinic every day of my March break. Suddenly the five hundred dollars didn't seem enough. But I couldn't think of any way to get out of it. I'd made a commitment and it was impossible to break. I couldn't risk the wrath of Dr T. Not with another year and three months of dental school to still complete.

Cursing myself for being an idiot, I resigned myself to having no March break. The burden of studying for third quarter exams seemed worse knowing I wouldn't be having a holiday afterwards. To make matters even more unbearable it seemed like over half the class was going away some-where down south. And I would be stuck at the clinic.

Dr T's refresher course for foreign dentists was actually quite lucrative. Before a dentist from another country could practice dentistry legally in Canada they first had to pass the National Dental Examining Board (NDEB) exams. The NDEB exams had three different components, a written, pre-clinical and clinical section. The exams were taken in order and you had to pass each one before you could proceed to the next. The pass rate was about fifty percent for the written component, thirty percent for the pre-clinical and a mere ten percent for the clinical section. The purpose of the NDEB exams was to protect the Canadian public from poorly trained foreign dentists. For an American-trained dentist the overall pass rate for all three exams was about eighty to ninety percent. This was consistent with the high standard of dental education and dental care in the United States. For a Romanian-trained dentist the success rate was about as high as winning the lottery.

Dr T's course was nothing more than a prep course for the NDEB exams. It was lucrative because tuition for the one-week course was about three thousand dollars. Every year they registered about twenty-five students for the clinical course and about thirty students for the pre-clinical course. I helped with the clinical course while a second year student helped out with the pre-clinical course. We were both just glorified gophers. My first task after the foreign dentists registered was to show them where their assigned storage lockers were. Some of them had never used a combination lock before. One female dentist from Poland was in tears trying to open hers. Out of the twenty-five registered I had to help almost twenty open their locks on the first day. For the remainder of the week I was frequently called upon to open their combination locks. The Polish dentist never was able to figure out how the lock worked. One day she even switched her lock with a Russian dentist. The chaos that resulted was practically a new cold war.

All together there were seven Americans, four Britons, one Egyptian, eight eastern Europeans, two Japanese and one each from Russia, South Africa and South Korea. During the week I became good friends with one of the American dentists. Pamela was originally Canadian but had graduated from dental school in Boston. Her dad had a successful practice in Toronto but she'd gone to school in the States since she couldn't get accepted to any dental schools in Canada. Unfortunately for her she was now stuck in United States until she could pass her NDEB exams.

I thought she had a good chance, along with two of the Brits and three other Americans. The others had a better chance of being elected Grand Pubah of the Royal Order of Water Buffaloes.

Most of the others were intimidated by the instructors, but since I was merely a helper, they came to me with their questions. "Am I doing this right? Is this how it will be on the NDEB exam?" It saddened me when I realized some had gone into debt to pay for the course. The Eastern Europeans were the most pathetic. They'd come to Canada with their dreams of becoming rich by practicing dentistry here. In reality the vast majority were dental butchers. They had been practicing brutal dentistry for years and their learned bad habits and rough skills were ingrained. In their own countries, local anesthetic was a rarity and used only for difficult extractions. Fillings, root canals and even simple extractions were all done without freezing. They had been forced to work at a quick and subsequently sloppy pace, just to scrape out a living. Worse yet, they knew nothing about the preventative aspects of dentistry. To turn them loose on the unsuspecting public would be even sadder than their own plight.

Some of the questions I was asked only indicated how out-to-lunch these people really were.

After a while they started to get on my nerves. They were all so eager for the easy way out, trying to weasel all the knowledge they could. As if they were entitled, simply by virtue of having paid their three thousand dollars. Most of them believed that the one-week course was all they needed to bring them up to our

Canadian standards. At least a solid year of instruction would be more realistic.

The second year student helping with the pre-clinical group told me even more incredible stories about his group of hopefuls. Supposedly there was a dentist from one of the newly independent African nations who had never seen a high-speed dental drill before. Ironically he was a very successful dentist in his country. Apparently there were almost no cavities there due to a lack of refined sugar in their diets. Over ninety-five percent of all his work was extracting teeth. And that he was very good at.

After the first few days my interest in helping out with the course was detoured by my interest in Pamela. She was a beautiful brunette with a shapely body and unbelievably emerald green eyes. When she looked at you,you couldn't help but feel she was really looking at you, looking down inside of you to your core. It was unsettling and yet sexual. As a fringe benefit of her beauty she never lacked for instruction. It seemed either Dr Thomsky, Dr Imanka or one of the other instructors was always in her cubicle, personally helping her.

Yet when she wanted to go for lunch or sit around and shoot the shit she came to me. I felt somewhat honored and even protective of her when we sat in the cafeteria. Especially when I saw Dr Thomsky sitting at a distant table giving Pamela the eye. During lunch on Thursday she asked me if I knew any good restaurants which I might recommend for dinner. As I named a few I wondered why she was asking since I didn't think she knew anyone in the city and I couldn't see her going out by herself.

Which made me ask,"Why don't you let me take you out to a great place tonight? Do you like seafood?" As I held my breath in anticipation, I realized that I'd just been craftily maneuvered into asking her out. She'd asked about the restaurants in such a meek, slightly down-trodden manner. She must have known I'd feel sorry for her. The bottom line was, I didn't give a shit if she had manipulated me. Especially since she took me up on my offer. We arranged to meet at seven thirty.

That night we had a wonderful time. Good conversation, a bottle of tart, crispy Mateus, fresh seafood and specialty coffees filled with potent Irish Whiskey. She asked me during the course of the meal if I knew of any place she could work out, since she was doing nothing but eating, studying and sleeping all week. I suggested she could come to my fitness club and we decided on a 7 pm workout the next day.

Lingering over our specialty coffees I was thinking of how to get her to invite me up to her hotel room. By now I was really falling for her. She was beautiful, smart, rich and best of all she seemed to enjoy my company. She paid for dinner despite my protests and we both hopped into a cab. The weather had taken a bizarre turn for the worse and it was snowing wildly. I didn't want to blow it so I gave the cab driver my address first. Pamela was cozying right up beside me in the cab and her proximity was driving me crazy. She wore Chloe and the rich fragrance was filling my senses. Arriving with a short skid in front of my apartment building I asked, "Do you want to come up for a coffee?" I was certain she would and I was totally deflated when she said, "No thanks, I'd like to do some studying tonight. But thanks for taking me to dinner. I'll see you tomorrow." With that she gave me a quick peck on the side of the cheek and the next thing I knew I was out of the taxi watching it slip, slide away. The red tail-lights were soon consumed by the ashen flurries.

What a major league disappointment. Obviously she thought of me as just a friend. Of course knowing that only made me want her more. That night I even dreamt of her. I'd never before fooled around on a girlfriend but Nancy and I had just started to go out and we weren't really serious yet. Besides it was just wishful thinking at this point. The next day after the course I met Pam at my fitness club at 7pm. She looked great in her gym clothes and I couldn't help but be proud that she was with me.

The fitness instructor, I think his name was Todd, helped Pam with almost every exercise. I'd worked out at his club, once or twice a week for the last seven months and he'd never helped me with any thing. In fact when I went to sign Pam into the club, he even asked me if I had a membership.

The look on Todd's arrogant face was priceless when she told him, " I know you must be very busy. I hope you don't mind if I work out with my friend Ken."

I was liking her more and more.

The extent of my feelings became embarrassingly noticeable later that afternoon. I was spotting her as she bench pressed,standing over her prone body watching her strain and groan as she brought the weight to her ample chest again and again. My shorts were only inches from her face. As she looked up at me I felt a familiar warmth as blood rushed to my groin. My shorts poked out in front of me like a pup tent. I quickly walked away and pulled my t-shirt over the offending growth, while trying to imagine my grandmother's vagina. I pretended that nothing had happened and I hoped that she hadn't noticed.

After we showered and changed at the club she asked me if I wanted to go out for dinner. I was confused because I didn't think she was interested in me, but then I realized she was probably just lonely and wanted some company. We went to a Mexican restaurant and washed down the hot and spicy food with bottle after bottle of icy cold Coronas. Afterwards she totally shocked me by inviting me back to her hotel room.

On the way there she told me she had to return to Chicago the next day for a friend's wedding. She'd be missing the last two days of the course. Which meant I had nothing to lose. Her room was on the seventh floor. As we rode the elevator I couldn't think of a thing to say. Just before the silence started to get prickly she said, " We're not going to have sex." "That's okay, I said, even though it wasn't. When we got to her room the first thing she did was give me a toothbrush and toothpaste. Even though I was insulted I didn't care because I knew that we were going to do something. As soon as I put the toothbrush down she was sticking her tongue down my throat.

Later that night we said our goodbyes. Neither of us made promises to keep in touch. I knew I would never see her again.

The last two days of the course dragged on without Pam there. On the last day Dr Thomsky asked me if I knew what had happened to Pam. I replied, " I believe she had to attend a friend's wedding in Chicago. " Dr Thomsky looked at me oddly for a moment, then winked and walked away.

After March break I felt oddly refreshed. I'd actually spent each and every day at the clinic from nine to five, yet I felt as if I'd had a holiday. Maybe it was my romantic interlude with Pam. More probably it was because I hadn't been working in the clinic. I'd spent a whole week there with no stress. I'd even had fun. Dr Thomsky and the other profs had treated me more as a human being than a mere student.

People who are afraid of spiders, or heights, or flying are often cured of their phobia by being exposed to what they fear most. My March break in the clinic seemed to desensitize me to the dental school environment. Psychologically I felt more comfortable and less intimidated. Which was great because the last quarter of third year was a battle to the very end. I needed as much help as I could muster both mentally and in practice. Clinically I was behind in only one subject. Operative dentistry. I still had another thirty-five surfaces of silver fillings to complete and only eight weeks left. I needed to finish almost five surfaces a week. I'd given up on calling Anna, the thirteen-year-old with wall-to-wall decay because she was too unreliable. I started a couple new patients in the last quarter that ultimately saved my ass.

Ron was a member of a motorcycle gang with definite underworld credentials. Every time I phoned him for an appointment I had to leave a message on The Clubs private line. The Club was a prominent member of the organized crime panthenon. Ron was six feet four and must have weighed at least three hundred pounds. In fact he was so heavy that my dental chair was incapable of lifting him. I had to put the chair to its proper height first and then get him to sit in it. The only time I tried to lift him from the chair motor, I thought I'd burned it out.

Ron and I made a special deal right from the start. I wouldn't charge him for any of the dental work he needed and he agreed to never cancel an appointment and always be on time. In the back of my mind I'd often imagine what Ron would do to me if he wasn't happy with my work. Break my kneecaps, snap all my fingers backwards. Even my instructors seemed a little intimidated by him.

Ron never took off his black leather jacket. Not once. Even when the temperature in the clinic rose into the eighties. Furthermore he always wore the same Black Sabbath,-black t-shirt under his leather jacket. With his long reddish blond hair and full beard he reminded me of a Viking warrior. I ended up completing thirty surfaces of silver fillings on Ron. He was always on time and he never missed a single appointment. It was difficult at times to get away without charging him but somehow I managed to pull it off. Ron's teeth were so large that I had to get a special matrix band from dental stores whenever I had to fill a molar. The first time Dr Imanka saw his teeth he got so excited he had to get his camera to take pictures. Dr Imanka said that they were the biggest teeth he'd ever seen. When I was filling them I had to use as much as six double spills of amalgam. The average filling took just a single spill of amalgam and sometimes two double spills.

When Ron stood up after the end of his first appointment Dr Imanka, who was standing at the edge of my cubicle, commented reverently, "You a BIG man!" Ron smiled. I smiled. Dr Imanka looked small.

The other patient I started in the fourth quarter was a petite dark haired graduate student named Nardeen. She was twenty-two and already had an undergraduate degree in physics. She was truly a peculiar person. Soon after she became my patient I started to receive odd notes in my dental cubicle. The first note said, "I want to feel you in my mouth! " The second, "Please fill me up, I need it bad." Finally she put a phone in my cubicle with instructions on what time my mysterious groupie would phone. To this day I have no idea how she was able to get the phone to work in the clinic. When she called it was almost 6 pm and the only other person in the clinic was a janitor. I picked up. "Hello, who is this?" I asked. " It's the love of your life,darling," she purred. I didn't recognize her voice at all. "What do you want?"" I want you, you silly man" "Do I know you?" I enquired. "Of course you do, you've been inside my mouth with your big tool."

she breathed, Suddenly I realized who it was. I still needed her to fulfill my third year operative dentistry requirements. "Nardeen, how are you ?" There was a long pause before she replied, "So do you want to do me?" I was flabbergasted. It took a while before I could stammer my response, " Nardeen, as much as I like you I'm not allowed to get involved with a patient. I could get kicked out of dental school." In reality she really was butt ugly and I would have rather had sex with one of The Golden Girls. She replied, "I promise I won't tell. Please..pretty please." I rationalized further, " Honestly, I find you very attractive, but I can't take the risk. You must understand."

"I won't be your patient then,"she sulked " Look, I'll make you a deal, when I'm all finished your dental work, you won't be my patient, and then we can get together." I offered. There was only the slightest pause before she said," Sounds good to me, I can hardly wait." I choked out, "Me too." And we said goodbye, but not before I set up our next dental appointment.

Not only was I able to finish my silver filling surfaces, I could also complete my inlay requirements with Nardeen. An inlay is a gold or porcelain filling that fits right inside a tooth. Inlays took two separate appointments. The first appointment was used to prepare the tooth, take an accurate impression of the tooth and then place a temporary filling on the tooth. At the next appointment the temporary was removed, the inlays were tried in and if they fit properly they were permanently cemented in place. With Nardeen I had to actually make the gold inlays in the lab. After our first appointment it took me a few days and a couple attempts to make the inlays fit. When I called Nardeen to set up our appointment so I could cement the inlays she pulled a cruel prank on me. She told me she had the temporary fillings removed by a "real dentist" (her words) and had the teeth filled in permanently with white fillings.I practically shit my pants. She let me out of my misery after a short time and told me she was kidding. I wasn't sure if I believed her and when I set up our appointment to cement the inlays, I had my doubts if she would show up. To my great relief she showed up for her appointment and I had the inlays checked off and permanently cemented in less than an hour. With Ron and Nardeen I was able to finish my operative dentistry requirements and just in the nick of time too. I had my last surface checked off on our last clinic day before our final exams.

We had a grand total of twelve final exams, so compared with second year it was a piece of cake. The only problem was that we had the twelve exams in the space of five days. I had to take sleeping pills to get to sleep and caffeine pills to wake up. Again it was a nightmare. The last exam was on a Friday and I started work the following Monday.

Every year the faculty of dentistry tried to provide as many jobs as possible to the senior students. There were the prestigious operative dentistry clinical positions as well as oral surgery and emergency clinic offerings as well as the few odd jobs. I got one of the odd jobs.

I was to work Monday to Friday, eight thirty to five assisting Ron who ran the dental stores.

The only requirement that Ron insisted on was that I never be late for work. Once I got to work Ron didn't care how hard or how fast I worked. In fact several times during the summer he took me aside and told me to slow down. We used to sit and talk for hours. Ron was a truly fascinating guy and I learned as much from him as I did from most of our profs. He told me what actually worked in private practice, not what we were taught in school. He had served many years in the army, and I was enthralled by his stories of life in the military. Best of all,though, were his stories of students past. Ron had a yearbook with pictures of all the past graduating classes in dentistry. We'd go through each year and he'd tell me all the really bizarre and weird stories.

I was amazed and shocked by all the suicides. There had been at least ten in only twenty years. Ron told me about the guy who lost his right hand while woodworking. He went back to school and became an actuary. Then there was Pulp Peters. He got his nickname from drilling through to the nerve or pulp in almost every filling he did. Some how he still graduated. I guess there was still hope for me.

Ron also told me about the woman dentist who had three children in her four years of dental school. To top it off she ended up being first in her class. There was also the scandal when three students had been kicked out for cheating. One of the students had even been the president of his class. Luckily they were allowed to return and graduated one year after all their class-mates. I think the best story I heard was about the student whose patient died in his dental chair. The patient had a heart condition and although the student was cleared of all wrong-doing, the student had a nervous breakdown and apparently never recovered. He still lives in an institutionalized setting. Another student had a heart attack and died during one of his practical exams. Many students married classmates and one of our profs even married a student from his classes.

I received a letter in mid August informing me that I had passed everything and I even ended up with five honors out of my twelve courses. I was ecstatic.

The rest of the summer passed quickly and I took a week off before I was to return to fourth year. My parents lent me their truck and Nancy and I drove up to our family cottage just outside Thunder Bay. The drive was almost twenty hours long. We had a great time at the cottage and we did all the touristy things there are to do in Thunder Bay. As the days melted away I began to feel fear and trepidation about returning to the dental school. I entertained the idea of staying at the cottage and never going back. My dreams were marbled with stress and more fear. I remember lying on the dock on our last night there and telling Nancy that I didn't want to go back to school. The stars were like jewels in the velvet sky and her eyes sparkled with hope. She told me that the year would be over before we knew it and that she loved me. I told her that I loved her too and some how the fears turned into gossamer threads that sublimated into the blackness.

Fourth Year

The clinical requirements we had in fourth year were quite different than the requirements we had in third year. In operative dentistry we had to complete sixty-five surfaces of silver fillings, fifteen white fillings and two practical exams. This didn't seem so bad compared to third year until we realized we had only half of the clinical time to finish all of it.

In third year we'd been assigned only one unit of fixed prosthodontics. For fourth year we were expected to complete ten whole units. These units would be the most difficult clinical requirements to fulfill in fourth year.

In removable prosthodontics we had to make a minimum of two separate upper and lower partial dentures. Endodontics was accumulative with third year. To graduate we would need a total of twelve successfully completed root canals.

As in third year we were responsible for the periodontal health of all our patients. Paedodontic and orthodontic requirements were basically the same as in third year.

Fourth year was also the year of the seminar. We had to present major seminars in paedodontics, oral medicine and orthodontics. Fortunately we had fewer lecture hours and in the fourth quarter we actually had no lectures at all. Theoretically if you finished all your clinical requirements you could finish fourth year by the beginning of the last quarter. It was a race to the finish line.

One student who wasn't in the race was Marcus. Third year had been too much for him.. He failed three academic subjects in his supplementals and didn't complete successfully his clinical requirements in both operative dentistry and fixed prosthodontics. Poor Marcus. But oddly enough he didn't seem too upset by his plight. He was allowed to return and repeat third year. So while we were all starting fourth year he was starting third year all over again. I think

I would rather have slit my wrists. By unspoken agreement the members of our class avoided contact with Marcus at all costs. It was almost as if he had a form of contagion that we all wanted to avoid. I think that we were all afraid of being seen with him by our instructors and being linked by association.

Our classes in fourth year were much more practically oriented and generally less academic. The most interesting course was psychology. Unfortunately all we had was a grand total of four hours in this subject. Three of these hours were theoretical and only one hour was about psychology as it applied to the field of dentistry. This seemed totally absurd to me, since every time a patient sat down in your dental chair, you had to use psychology. Instinctively you sized up their current mental state. Were they simply terrified or just a little tense or completely relaxed? If they were nervous how did you calm them down? Should you tell patients you were going to give them a needle or just sneak up on them and do it.

These were all aspects of applied psychology that we were never taught. All of us worked through these problems with varying degrees of success, I knew some people in our class would have a rough time when they graduated, because they had no people skills at all. They might have been technically excellent with their hands but they had no idea what to say to people or how to treat them.

Instinctively I seemed to know how to relate to people well. I remembered stuff that patients bad told me months before. When patients talked I actively listened. I asked them questions about their families, their jobs and their interests. And I asked because I was actually curious. I really wanted to know.

People can tell a phony. I listened to other students talking to patients and I would cringe.

They either talked down to them or ignored them. There was absolutely no rapport. I found it kind of sad.

My favorite patient in fourth year was also the most important. Susan was in her late thirties but looked younger. She had a boy, twelve,and a girl, nine. She lived with her husband and their two children on a farm just outside the boundaries of the city. She stayed at home as a housewife and her husband was in the last year of a three-year nursing program.

Things must have been quite challenging for them financially because during the three years he was in school they had very little income coming into the household. Despite their economic status,or more likely because of it, Susan was coming to the clinic to have her dental work done. She needed two separate, three-unit bridges. That was sixty percent of my requirements for fixed prosthodontics.

I don't think I've ever met a nicer person than Susan.Anywhere- Ever. She was always in a good mood. I'd phone her up for the umpteenth time and tell her that we needed yet another umpteenth plus one appointment. She never complained. Not once. On top of that she was always bringing me little gifts and presents. She would even phone me before my exams and wish me good luck.She never missed a single appointment and she was never late.

In total it took twenty-five appointments or roughly seventy-five hours in the clinic to finish Susan's two bridges. In a private dentist's office they would have cost her about three thousand dollars and it would have taken roughly six hours to do the work. At our clinic it cost her only six hundred dollars, which made my renumeration about eight dollars an hour, compared to five hundred dollars an hour in private practice. -

Her bridges were an exercise in frustration right from the start. So many times I had to repeat clinical procedures and in some cases I even had to go backwards in time. Susan was missing two teeth, a lower right premolar and an upper right premolar. The idea of the bridges was to fill the spaces of the missing teeth by attaching a fake tooth to crowns on either side of the spaces. I made a huge mistake in trying to do both bridges at more or less the same time. Both the top teeth and bottom teeth were prepped before I had cemented either bridge in permanently. I took my final impressions of both top and bottom before the Christmas holiday. Susan had a strong gag reflex and every impression had been almost torture for her. We slaved and sweated to get the impressions, doing about twenty before we got it right.

When I returned from Christmas holiday the impressions were no longer good because the teeth had shifted significantly in the three week time period. When I told Susan that we had to redo the impressions, I thought she was going to cry. I thought I was going to cry. Luckily from all our experience it only took us four appointments to get the impressions again. From there it was relatively easy because we sent our impressions to a commercial dental laboratory, and they were the ones who actually fabricated the bridges. The appointments went something like this;

1.-Clean teeth, get periodontal approval to proceed.
2.-Take preliminary impressions of top and bottom teeth
3.-Start occlusal adjustment to reshape teeth to give Susan a better bite
4.-Finish occlusal adjustment
5.-Start preparing upper teeth for upper bridge
6.-Continue
7:-Finish preparing upper teeth
8.-Start preparing lower teeth for lower bridge.
9.-Finish preparing lower teeth
10.-Attempt final impression of upper teeth
11.-Continue
12.-Successful final impression of upper teeth
13.-Attempt final impression of lower teeth
14.-Continue
15.-Successful final impression of lower teeth
Christmas Holiday
16.-Retake impression for upper teeth
17.-Retake impression for lower teeth
18.-Attempt to get final bite record
19.-Successful bite record
Bridges fabricated in commercial dental laboratory
20.-Try in upper bridge, cement temporarily

21.-Permanently cement upper bridge, adjust occlusion

22.-Try in lower bridge, cement temporarily

23.-Permanently cement lower bridge, start to adjust occlusion

24.-Finish adjusting occlusion

25.- Polish bridges and receive final credit for six units

AMEN !

By the time I had finished with Susan I felt as if we were family. What we had started October 10th, was finally done by March 5th. I knew Susan's dog's name, (Mork),her two cats' names,(Nimbus and Sam). I even knew what her children wanted to do when they grew up, (astronaut and nurse).

Susan had gone through hell with me. Hours and hours with her mouth open, impression after impression, appointment after appointment. It was actually a sad moment when we said our final good-byes.

I could count myself lucky for having had such an excellent patient. Others in the class didn't fare as well. My friend Dave, had a patient quit after ten appointments on a four-unit bridge. The patient was fed up with all his time being wasted and ended up going to a private dentist to have the bridge finished. Dave was screwed,he ended up getting no credit at all for the work he had done. Dave was despondent.

I invited Dave over to my apartment for a little therapy afterwards. I sat him down and picked up the phone. I blocked my number, called Dave's patient's number and let it ring. I looked up his patient's number earlier that day from Administration. A woman answered the phone. "Hello is this the home of Gord Smith ?" I asked. There was a slight pause and rather hesitantly she replied,"Yes." "Well, this is the desk clerk at the Ambassador Hotel (a dive known locally as the Bare Ass Love Hotel), your husband has left his credit card in his room and I'm just calling so he can come down and pick it up at the front desk. Have a great day ma'am." Next I called Pizza Pizza, blocking my number once again. I put in an order for two large pizzas for Mr Gord Smith for delivery. Double anchovies, extra hot peppers-extra cheese and pepperoni.

But I wasn't done yet. I called Mutual Life and made an appointment for the following Monday at 6 pm to discuss whole life policies with an agent, I requested that the agent be fluent in Urdu. My last call was to a ReMax office to discuss selling my home (I claimed that my wife and I were breaking up.) I made the appointment for 7 pm the following Monday. This time I asked for an agent who was fluent in Mandarin.

Since I knew the patient's address I asked Dave if he wanted me to place a sign on Mr Smith's front lawn that said CRACK HOUSE "Holy shit,Ken, I sure don't want to get on your wrong side.

" Dave laughed. We started laughing and we couldn't stop. My therapy was the perfect medicine and every time Dave and I ran into each other for the next few days we'd start to chuckle.

Another luckless student had his patient die just before he was to deliver the hapless man's denture. It was terrible because every step of the denture had been completed except for the final delivery. After several discussions with Dr Keller from the removable prosthodontics department, the funeral director and the dead man's relatives, the student was able to insert the dentures in the dead man's mouth with Dr Keller present and actually receive full credit for the case. It was definitely the most bizarre denture delivery I'd ever heard of.

Other students in our class had tough times finishing their cases for fixed prosthodontics. My friend Paul had started a six-unit anterior bridge in mid October. It wasn't until the first week in May that Paul finally cemented the bridge in permanently. Paul nicknamed his case, "The Bridge Too Far" at first, later it was "The Bridge over the River SUCK"and then eventually."The Bridge From HELL." The case started to go bad in January. Paul had submitted the final impressions and bite records to Dr Grant for approval to have the case fabricated in the lab. He left the case for Dr Grant on a Friday afternoon. By Monday afternoon the case was back in Paul's cubicle with a note from Dr Grant. Paul had forgotten to put the shade of white he wanted the bridge to be, on the lab requisition slip. Paul wrote the shade down and put it back in Dr Grant's office for approval that same afternoon.

On Friday it was back in Paul's cubicle with a new note. Paul had to take new impressions and bite records since it had been too long, and the teeth had probably shifted, necessitating new impressions. It took Paul another two weeks to get new impressions. He put his case back in Dr Grant's office to get approval and three days later it was back in Paul's cubicle with another note. Paul's impressions were unacceptable and Dr Grant wanted Paul to take new impressions. Back and forth Paul's case went between Dr Grant's office and Paul's cubicle, until the end of April and Paul realized that Dr Grant had become his worst nightmare. To make matters worse, Paul's patient, Tim, was unsympathetic. Tim was from Nova Scotia and he threatened Paul that he was going to go back and have the bridge finished by his old family dentist. Paul was getting squeezed from all sides. He needed help.

Help came in the form of a dental convention in Arizona. Dr Grant attended the convention for a whole week and Paul was able to get his case approved by another instructor. When he permanently cemented the bridge, Paul was ecstatic. That night Paul, Vijay, Dave, and I went to a local watering hole to celebrate. Paul got wasted and ended up going a little crazy. He asked a girl to dance. She took one withering look at him and said, "No." Paul didn't back down. With his best fuck you look he attacked, In about two months from now I'm going to be a DENTIST, but you're still going to be working at your same dead-end job, you're going to marry some loser guy, you'll have a couple of ugly, stupid kids, and if you're lucky, after saving and scrimping for five years you might be able to take your kids to Disney World. And by the way you're always going to be fat and ugly." The look on her face was priceless. I thought she was going to claw his eyes out. For a while I thought her and her group of friends were going to lynch him. The bouncer came over to see if things were okay. They weren't and we all got kicked out. We laughed our asses off all the way home. Close to Paul's apartment we found a stray grocery cart. Paul was having trouble walking he was so wasted, so we put him in the grocery cart and rolled him to his door. He was totally passed out so we just left him like that. Asleep, on his front door step, poured into a grocery cart.

For rotations in fourth year we had two weeks in oral surgery, two weeks in the emergency clinic and of course our sporadic and apparently random assignments in the paedodontic clinic.

In oral surgery, now that we were in fourth year we were expected to take more of an active role in the procedures. Instead of just freezing the patient and letting someone else do the actual extractions, now the roles were reversed. My first rotation in oral surgery was in the second week of October. As always it was a welcome break from having to phone and schedule regular patient appointments.

Nurse Watson looked as lovely as ever, all two hundred and fifty pounds. Of course she had her ubiquitous diet coke with her, on her desk. I wasn't afraid of her anymore because I realized she had no real power. It was all illusion. The only thing she did was book your patients. She had no role in the deciding of marks. Marks were where the real power was.

Oddly enough I think Nurse Watson actually liked me. On Wednesday afternoon after we'd finished with our patients she let myself and a couple third year students fool around with the nitrous oxide. (laughing gas). She brought us into one of the operatories where the nitrous was hooked up and showed us how to use the gas. I went first. I put the gas mask on my face and one of the third year students adjusted the flow rate, so I was breathing one hundred percent oxygen. Slowly he started adding nitrous oxide to the mix until I was breathing sixty percent nitrous and forty percent oxygen.

The nitrous had a slightly sweet odor that smelt oddly familiar. I first felt a light-headedness and then my outer extremities, fingers and toes, began to tingle. Everything around me appeared bigger, as if the normal physical dimensions of reality were being stretched like the skin of an inflating balloon. As I continued to breathe in the sweet gas I felt even more light-headed. When my lips started to go numb things got a little weird. A strong euphoric feeling washed over me and I felt I was on the verge of remembering something important. The intensity of feeling was so strong that I had to stop. The deja vu feeling washed away like rain in the desert and I was left with a slight headache that lasted for a few hours. What a rush. In my first dental practice I was going to make sure that I had nitrous oxide gas.

Just before the end of first quarter we were each assigned a topic for a seminar in pediatric dentistry. It was to be a seminar with a twist. We'd be presenting the seminars at the homes of our pediatric profs in small groups. The idea was to create a feeling of camaraderie between us and them.

The seminars ended up being a sort of slow torture rather than a sharing of kinship. I just knew that I was going to go to either Dr Flood's or Dr Yank's home. I was right. Just before Christmas, myself, Dave W. and six other students were cordially invited to attend at the home of Dr Flood.

From the outside Dr Flood had a stately two-story, red, brick Georgian style home. The neighborhood was an exclusive area which only added to the grandeur of the home. Dave W and I were the first students to arrive. After ringing the doorbell and hearing a muffled chime we waited about a half minute before Dr Flood answered the door and invited us in. He looked kind of funky in an old pair of denim blue jeans and a blue, button down oxford shirt. In contrast Dave and I were wearing long sleeve white dress shirts, dress pants and ties.

We were escorted from the grand entranceway, past an enormous kitchen into a cozy-looking living room. Everything was done in an African motif. There were masks all over the place. In between the masks were the heads of gazelles, antelopes and other unknowable animals. I felt like we were on safari. Dave and I sat at opposite ends of a buttery-soft, brown, leather couch. I imagined myself saying, "Nice place, when are the Zulus attacking? Dr Flood stood impotently in front of us and asked us if we wanted a beer. Dave and I replied in perfect unison "Yes please." Dr Flood smiled in his creepy, 'what is wrong with this picture' Afrikaner grin and left the room to get us our drinks. Dave and I looked at each other. "Nice place eh?" I said to him.

"Yeah, I wonder where he keeps the dead bodies?"

In front of us was a coffee table with food on it. At least I think it was supposed to be food. There were two big bowls, one with a brown mush and the other with a beige colored mush and a plate with pita bites. They were hummus and baba ganouche. At the time I had never tried either and I didn't even know what they were. I tried both and found the hummus to be especially tasty. The garlic was overpowering and now I knew what gave Dr Flood his unique aroma. Eventually all the students arrived. I finished my beer in the first two minutes and started looking around for another. There were no others. We all got one drink, and no more. What a cheap bastard!

Once we were all seated Dr Flood asked who would like to start. There were no takers. The silence was starting to become anxiety provoking. I found my throat getting dry and my pulse racing. "How about you, Ken?" he asked innocently. I wanted to say,"No thanks, I think I'd rather admire your decorating." But instead I replied,"Sure I'll start."

I stood up to speak and looking at my cue cards I began. Every second or third sentence I was interrupted by Dr Flood. I had researched my topic extensively and I felt I had a good grasp and understanding of what I was presenting. Dr Flood's interruptions were more like he was heckling and I was starting to feel myself getting angry. Just when I was about to say, "Fuck you!" he stood up and left the room. I was about halfway through my fifteen minute presentation and without Dr Flood there, the rest went very smoothly. I was asking, "Any questions?" when he returned. There were no questions and I sat down to rest.

Dr Flood said, "Ken, you do realize that this was a seminar and not a reading exercise? I am going to have to penalize you for reading most of your report rather than presenting it in a seminar fashion." I had small cue cards which I had written short form notes. It was impossible to read from short form notes. I felt like whipping all the cue cards at him one by one. Instead I said, "Maybe if you stayed for my whole seminar you would have seen I wasn't reading my report." There was a preternatural silence in the room. The only sound was the tick-tock of the grandfather clock in the corner. I saw the end of my dental career right there and then. Unexpectedly Dr Flood started to laugh,"Actually your report was well researched and overall it was not bad." I'd survived.

The rest of the evening I just sat back and watched with great glee the discomfort of my fellow students. Dr Flood spared no one with his heckling and obnoxious interruptions. One of the female students was practically in tears by the time he was done with her. By the time the last seminar was presented we were all ready to leave.

Before we could go, Dr Flood shared an amusing story with us. One of his friends went to dental school in Cleveland Ohio. A prescription pad was stolen from the main clinic there. About a week later the director of the dental clinic received a strange call. It was from a local pharmacist. He had a very tall, very muscular, very black man with a very odd prescription that was from the school's dental clinic. Apparently the prescription was for, "Two pounds Mo-Feen." We were all laughing so hard I started to cry.

Instead of going straight home, Dave and I decided to go out to a downtown bar and have a few beers. Afterwards Dave dropped me off at Nancy's apartment so I could spend the night. Nancy and I were together almost every night now. She was my cure for the dental clinic.

I was living in the same two-story luxury apartment from third year. My roommate Dan had moved out to a one-bedroom love nest for himself and his girlfriend. My new roommate was Ed. He was a first year science student whose ultimate goal in life was to make a hundred thousand dollars a year. His Korean parents owned a variety store in a nearby city. Ed spoke with a Korean accent and sometimes was hard to understand. All year long the only things I saw him eat were hot dogs and chocolate bars. He went home every weekend to help with the store and came back every Sunday night with more hot dogs and choc-olate bars. His parents practically stroked out when they saw Nancy in her bath-robe, right out of the shower. They couldn't believe that their son was living in such a sinful environment. In his quest for a "Hundid tousand dollars a hair" he encountered many people. There was the guy in his biology class who told him about an actuary student who made one hundred k the first year after graduating. I told him about a guy who graduated from dental school who made (you guessed it) a hundred k, his first year out. He was obsessed.

Ed was the worst at taking phone messages. When anyone called for me, he'd pick up the phone, listen for a few seconds, then say, "Ken's not here." and hang up all in the span of about five seconds. But the great thing about Ed was that he kept to himself. I could go for days without seeing him. The entire time I stayed with him he never got a single phone call. It was actually kind of weird. I'm not sure what Ed eventually did with his life, but I sincerely hope he is making a hundred thousand dollars a year.

Being in fourth year had certain advantages. The profs were starting to treat us more as colleagues and less like students. The administrative staff was nicer and the students from the lower years looked up to us in envy and esteem. The other years seemed pretty similar to our year in that the majority of the students were arrogant jerks. Unlike other faculties we never engaged in team sports or intramurals. I think all of us were afraid of damaging our hands. One of the guys in our class told a story about his father. His father was a successful dentist and every year took his family to Whistler to go skiing. One year he lost control on a steep trail and was heading right for a tree. Rather then put his hands out to break his fall, he hit the tree directly with his chest. His hands were fine but he broke four ribs. And after that he took the family to Florida instead of skiing.

In between third and fourth year one of my patients had died. He drove his transport truck into the wall of an overpass on the 401. His body was so badly burned that they couldn't identify him without using dental records. It was in September when the RCMP officer came to the dental school to make a positive identification. I was called from an afternoon lecture to the main dental clinic. I had no idea what it was about and when they introduced me to the grim faced lieutenant I thought I was in big trouble. I just didn't know what I'd done wrong.

He was carrying a small wooden box, that contained the mandible of the man burned in the crash. My heart-beat returned to a normal rhythm when he told me why he was there. We had to take x-rays of the teeth in the mandible and compare it to the x-rays I had on file. At that point the officer's demeanor changed and he became quite kind. He told me that he really appreciated my help and that he was sorry to have to subject me to the identification process. He opened up the box and the room was inundated with the smell of a campfire. The mandible was intact but charred. We took it to the x-ray machine and took the necessary x-rays. When we compared my old x-rays to the new ones, there was no doubt. The teeth were identical. The officer made me sign a mountain of paperwork attesting to the true identity of the crash victim. He thanked me and apologized once again. It was sad because the patient had been one of my favorites. I was torn between the emotions of sadness and gratefulness that I had been able to help.

Now that we were in fourth year we had an awesome responsibility. It was our turn for skit night. It was finally our chance to humiliate, embarrass and degrade our instructors in the most politically incorrect and tasteless way possible. It was up to us to set a new standard of gross deprivation.

We did a skit of Dental School Jeopardy, The audience was warmed up from the toothless efforts of the first, second and third year classes. The third year class had done a great spoof of Imanka's Project Dental Runway.

Our host Pres Johnson posed as Alex Trebeck. "Welcome everyone to tonight's exciting episode of Dental School Jeopardy. Say hello to our three contestants, Dr Willis, Dr Moore and Dr Imanka."

Dr Willis was played by Paul. He wore a skin-tight bald wig and a fur coat and sported a huge fake gold watch along with gold rings on every finger, Dan was Dr Moore.. To play Dr Moore Dan knelt down so that his eyes were barely visible over the top of the podium. One of the Army Guys played Dr Imanka. He wore super-nerdy,-coke bottle bottom glasses that made his eyes look enormous. As well he carried a huge paunch and held a beer bottle in his right hand. Johnson made the introductions. "Tonight I'd like you to meet our first contestant, Dr Willis is a certifiable psychopath whose hobbies include dreaming of driving a corvette again some-day, sodomizing underprivileged children and flirting with disaster. Please give a warm welcome to Dr Willis.

Next we have Dr Moore. Dr Moore, are you there? I can't see you, ah there you are Dr Moore, could you please stay on your tippy toes, so I can see you. Dr Moore loves to dress in women's clothes and shops regularly at the Mennonite thrift shop. He says he can't wait to compete today because, in his words, I want to show that mother-fricking, cock-sucking Dr Imanka that I'm smarter than him.

And finally let me introduce Dr Imanka. Dr Imanka was born in Japan but still doesn't know how to use chopsticks. When he was in high school he was voted-most likely to end up a convicted felon in prison with a cell-mate named Baba. Dr Imanka is our previous Dental School Jeopardy winner and has so far won twenty-three dollars and sixteen cents.

Our categories tonight are Smegma, Penis Envy, Therapists, Entre-nous and Women's Fashions. Dr Imanka you have the board." "Alex I'll take magma for two hundred dollars." 'I'm sorry Dr Imanka, the category is not magma, it is smegma, the smelly cheese like substance that lies underneath the foreskin." "Yeah that's okay, I'll take smegma for two hundred dollars." "Contestants, the answer is two pounds. Who knows this one? Yes Dr Moore?" "What is how much smegma I ate for breakfast?" " No Dr Moore that answer is incorrect, probably true but nevertheless incorrect. " " Does any-one else care to wager an answer? Ah yes, Dr Imanka?" "What is the amount of smegma that is stuck up Dr Moore's anus? "

" Yes Dr Imanka you are absolutely correct. Two hundred points for you. And once again you have control of the board.." Alex I'll take the rapists for five hundred dollars." "Okay then, contestants, the answer is, necrophiliacism. Does anyone care to wager a guess? Yes, Dr Willis?" I think the question is something you do for fun." "No Dr Willis that is incorrect, but you are very close to the right answer. Ah yes Dr Moore,what is your best guess?" "What is something Dr Willis's mother does for fun? " "No that may be true, Dr Moore, but that is not the correct answer. I'm sorry,contestants, we have run out of time. The proper response is, what all three of you like to do for fun. Next category, Dr Imanka, please."

"Alex, I'll take Penis Envy for two hundred dollars" "The answer here gentlemen is two and a half inches when erect." "Ah yes, Dr Imanka?" " I saw this once on national geographic, the answer is, the average size of a mountain gorilla's penis. " "No I'm sorry, Dr Imanka,that is not the right answer. Anyone else,........Anyone? Dr Moore? What is the average size of an adult male penis.?"That too is incorrect, doesn't any one know the answer to this one?, Ah Yes Dr Willis? " "Alex I'm going to go out on a limb here and say, what is the size of Dr Moore's penis? " " I'm sorry, all of you have given incorrect responses. The proper question is, what is wishful thinking for all three of you. Dr Imanka you still have control of the board." " Alex I'll take women's fashions for five hundred dollars. " "The answer is latex gloves. Who would like to venture a guess? Yes Dr Willis?" "What is, what I wear on a first date." "No, I'm sorry Dr Willis, that is incorrect." Ah yes Dr Moore, you have an answer?" "What is what the doctor wears when he does a rectal exam? " "Yes, Dr Moore, that is absolutely correct, you now have five hundred dollars and control of the board." "Alex. I'll take your daughter for two hundred dollars." "Dr Moore that is not one of our categories. Try again please." "Okay, I'll take the fricking French category for four hundred dollars." "I'm sorry Dr Moore, the category is actually Entre nous. " "Alright Alex, you turd burglar, I'll take Entre nous for four hundred dollars." "Listen, Dr Moore, you are a little, little insignificant man. One more inappropriate comment like that and you'll be off the show. Do you understand? " "Yeah, yeah,Alex, can we get on with the game?"

" Very well then, the answer is menage et trois. I'll be looking forward to your answer on this one Dr Moore. Ah yes Dr Moore, what is your response?" "Alex it's what I did with your wife and a spatula last night." "Dr Moore I've warned you.

I've had enough of your stupid, inane comments. You are truly an idiot. Security, would you please escort Dr Moore from the stage. Dr

Imanka you have an answer? " "Yes, if you break down the phrase you have, men age at rois, and rois in French means kings, therefore what is, men age at kings." "Dr Imanka I'm sorry,that is the most ridiculous question I have ever heard. Your logic is that of a moron. Dr Willis do you have any idea what the correct response is? "Well,Alex, let me think, I've never been very good at French, or even English, my first language is speaking in tongues. What is, a guy having sex with two hot babes." "Yes, you are indeed correct Dr Willis, you now have four hundred dollars and control of the board.

"Alex, I'll take women's fashion for five hundred dollars. " "Ah, Dr Willis, you've hit our daily double. You may bet up to seven hundred dollars." "Well Mr Trebek, I'll put   put my two cents in here and..." "Very well then. Dr Willis; you have bet two cents, the answer is thirty six DD." "Yeah that's a tough one Alex, what is Dr Imanka's waist measurement?" " Dr Willis, good try, the correct response is, what is Playboy's ideal breast measurement for their centerfolds. You now have three hundred and ninety-nine dollars and ninety-eight cents, and you still have control of the board."

"Alex, I'll take entre nous for six hundred dollars." "Okay, doctors, the answer is, poutine. Does any one care to wager a guess? Yes Dr Imanka, if you get this one right you will be in the lead." " I know, I know, I know this one, what is the leader of the Soviet Union? " "No, that is incorrect Dr Imanka. You really are mentally deficient, aren't you? Dr Willis, any ideas on this one?" "Well Alex, what is when your teenager has uncontrollable diarrhea?" "No I am sorry Dr Willis, you are not even close. The correct question is, what is French fries covered in cheese curds and gravy. And now gentlemen, it is time for Final Jeopardy. Our category tonight is Deviant Sexual Practices. What wagers will you be making tonight,doctors?"

"Alex, since I'm in the lead I'm going to bet ten dollars and five cents." "Dr Willis, your strategy is mind-numbingly stupid. Dr Imanka, how much would you care to wager for our Final Jeopardy question? " "I think I can honestly say that I know a lot about this category. I'd like to bet one hundred and ninety nine dollars."

"Very well,gentlemen, you will have thirty seconds to write down your final answer. Our Final Jeopardy question for tonight is, What is the number one pick up line at a gay bar?"

Time is up gentlemen. The correct answer is, may I push in your stool? Let's see what you've written down, Dr Imanka. It looks like, ask Dr Willis, he'll know the answer. " "No, I'm sorry Dr Imanka, that is not the correct response. You now have one dollar. Dr Willis, may we see your answer? May I sodomize you? Judges, judges, it looks like they'll accept your answer. Dr Willis,you are our Jeopardy winner for tonight with a grand total of four hundred and ten dollars and five cents.

I'd like to thank our audience, I hope you've enjoyed our show."

The applause was thundering. We even got a standing ovation from the student audience, but not our instructors. Did we cross the line? Maybe, but we had a hell of a good time doing it!

Operative dentistry in fourth year was really just a continuation of third year, except now we were expected, to work both faster and better. We also had two practical exams. One was for a multiple surface filling appointment and the other was for a filling with more than one pin in it. Both were about the most stressful exercises that we ever had to do in dental school. The most important aspect of operative dentistry was to never let them see you sweat, and always pick the nicest instructor you could.

What could be a routine appointment could turn into a complete nightmare if you had the wrong instructor. Dr Imanka and Dr Smith were the only two instructors I would work with. I had worked with Dr Guest before in third year and each time it was a disaster. Unfortunately, once in fourth year,before I had a chance to bring Dr Imanka over, Dr Guest stuck his pedunculated head into my cubicle. I took one look at his ugly face and knew I was in trouble. The whole appointment he wouldn't stop riding my ass. No matter what I did, it wasn't right and every time I tried to correct my deficiency, I just made things worse. At ten minutes to five he told me to speed up since he absolutely needed to be out of the clinic by five. That was fine with me because once I had checked the bite I would be finished. With Dave as my witness I asked Dr Guest if I needed to adjust the bite. He said," Take off half a millimeter and bring me back. If you take off more than half a millimeter I'll have to fail you. It was only a couple minutes later when Dr Guest flew back into my cubicle. With a quick glance at the prep he disdainfully declared, " Mister Spaldane you have obviously drilled deeper than a half millimeter. I'm going to have to fail you for your final prep. He was rising from the chair when I said," I don't think so Dr Guest." His puzzled look was worth a million dollars to me. Before Dr Guest could say anything I said," I'm not sure what the protocol is here, but I think I would be safe in assuming that I won't be failed for today's work. Dave is my witness, and he will attest to the fact that I didn't adjust the bite at all.

Dr Guest looked like he was going to explode. He reluctantly gave me a passing grade and he was out of the clinic with minutes to spare. And that was the last time I ever had to work with Dr Guest.

One early afternoon after my patient had cancelled I went home and suddenly had this great inspiration.

I called Dr Guest at his office. It was time to give Dr Guest a taste of his own medicine. His crime was unnecessary cruelty to students. His punishment was a prank call. I call blocked my number. After a couple rings, his receptionist answered, " Dr Guest's office. How may I help you today?". I said," I would like to speak to Dr Guest." The receptionist asked,"What is it about?" I told her,"He worked on my wife when she was pregnant and now she lost the baby because of what he did! I'm going to sue his ass." His receptionist sounded frazzled. "What is your wife's name?" "I don't want to talk to you. I want to speak to the dentist. RIGHT NOW," I bellowed, "Just a minute, sir." She put me on hold with Greensleeves playing in the background. About thirty seconds later he was on the line,"Hello, what seems to be the problem,sir," his voice cooed."You worked on my wife, she lost her baby because of you, and now I'm going to sue your cadaverous ass. The next time you hear from me it will be through my lawyer." I hung up the phone. I hope he lost some sleep because of my call. I knew it was a terrible thing to do, but he had totally terrorized me and many others in the clinic.

I waited until the third quarter to do my first practical exam. I had five surfaces of filling to do in three hours.My patient was a great guy. He was a forty-five-year-old unemployed auto-worker and he was very easy to work on. He could open his mouth so wide that I felt I could almost crawl right inside there. His name was Brent and he showed up fifteen minutes early for his appointment. I brought him in early and froze him before the instructors had arrived. I grabbed Dr Imanka as soon as he walked into the clinic and told him I wanted to do my practical exam. He came into the cubicle, said Hi to Brent, looked at the x-rays, looked quickly in his mouth and told me to proceed. I was nervous but determined to do a good job. When I went to Dr Imanka to have my rubber dam placement checked off, he was deep in conversation with Paul. Paul had obtained a so-called menu from a legal brothel in Nevada, from over the internet. Dr Imanka and Paul were laughing about some of the services. I had never seen Dr Imanka look so happy."Dr Imanka, would you like to check my rubber dam?" I asked. Dr Imanka said, "No that's okay Ken, get started and call me back when you've finished your preps."

Half an hour later I had cleaned out all the decay in Brent's teeth and had finished the preps. Looking over my cubicle wall I looked around for Dr Imanka. He was still talking and laughing. with Paul. I went over to Dr Imanka and asked him, " Could you please come and check my preps?"I asked. He replied, "Ah yes, Ken." He came over and looked carefully at my preps. He said, "Very good Ken, now please it is your turn to fill the teeth. Call me back when the teeth are filled, the rubber dam is off and you have checked the occlusion." He walked out of the cubicle and then beckoned me over. Once we were out of earshot of my patient he asked me quite seriously," What does this, around the world, mean?" I knew, but I couldn't see myself explaining it to my professor. "Sorry sir, I have no idea." I avoided eye contact with the good doctor and went right back to my cubicle to finish the fillings.

By this time my nervousness had dissipated through the pores of my effort and to my surprise I was finished in about forty-five minutes. When I brought Dr Imanka back to my cubicle for the final check I felt triumphant. I ended up with two Goods (G's) for my efforts. That day I felt like I was on cloud nine. Of course it didn't take long to bring me down to earth.

The next day I was working on my partial denture case with Dr Keller. The patient was a small Scottish woman, Betty, who insisted on calling me laddy. I was taking the final impressions for her partial. They were tricky because I was using a gooey material that typically ended up everywhere but where it was supposed to go.. Even though my patient wore a dental bib, I still spilled a little of the goo on the collar of her shirt.

Dr Keller went ape shit when he saw what I had done. He walked me far enough away from my cubicle, so Betty couldn't hear ." Listen to me Ken, I have to fail you for today because of your messiness. That stain on the collar of your patient's shirt won't come out. Her shirt is ruined because of your clumsiness." As Dr Keller walked away, he let loose with a stream of uncontrolled flatulence.

I was trying my hardest not to laugh, but when he rounded the corner of C Row I finally burst out laughing. Betty said,"My, that man farts a lot." I concurred,"Betty, he's the king of farts. I'm going to have to buy you a new shirt. I spilled some impression material on it, and it won't come out. She replied,"Oh laddy, don't you worry about this old thing, I know a few tricks with the wash." She was right, next time I saw her she was wearing the same shirt and there was no sign of a stain at all.

When I was finished with Betty's partial denture she presented me with a knitted Icelandic sweater. " Laddy, I want you to have this, for all you had to put up with, that terrible farting man, and all,"she said. I held the sweater in my hands and looked at the label. It read, Made by Betty, with LOVE "Oh Betty," I exclaimed, "This is so beautiful. Thank you very much!" Her smile with her brand new partial denture was worth a million dollars to me.

Sometimes the patient waiting room looked like the Jerry Springer Show. The patients who were normal sat huddled in the corners avoiding eye contact with the other patients. Drug deals went down and dates were made.

At other times the waiting room looked like a normal dentist's office. There was no rhyme or reason to its human...fluctuations, although some of us put stock in the lunar phases. It seemed that during full moons, the waiting room was absolutely chock full of loony tunes. We all had our share of bizarre patients.

My complete denture patient, Dorothy, had her brother drive her to her appointments. One cool day in the middle of November her brother had no jacket and no shirt. He sat in the waiting room completely shirtless. I was stunned. There was snow on the ground and he was shirtless.

One of Vijay's patients was a remarkably, beautiful young woman. She always wore miniskirts and no panties. When Vijay worked on his patient, the dental chair was tilted back in such a way that you could see everything. And I mean everything. She must have known what she was doing just by the shear volume of guys that stood over Vijay's cubicle. It didn't surprise us when she was recognized, working as a stripper at one of the city's strip clubs. I had been either walking or riding the bus for the last three and a half years. I knew I was going to need a car when I graduated. I asked my parents for a loan and they agreed to loan me up to five thousand dollars for a car. I put the word out that I was looking for a car. A couple weeks later I was approached by another student in my class.

Jimmy Chueng had a 1982 gold Jetta that he wanted to sell, so he could upgrade. It was a beautiful car and Jimmy had maintained it anally. It looked pretty sporty, it had a cool sun-roof and it was built like a tank. The engine purred like a contented pussycat. And he was only asking four thousand dollars for it. It was a done deal. It was great to have the freedom. I still took the bus to school, but it was wonderful to be able to go anywhere at anytime. I even took Nancy to the drive-in theater one night. We watched a double bill of Jaws and Jaws2. We actually both fell asleep before the second movie started. School was exhausting for her as well as me.

I no longer had to take the Greyhound bus to get back to my home town. I'd met a lot of strange people over the years on the bus. Most memorable was the guy who tried to get me to loan him a thousand dollars so he could get the big score. He never told me what the big score was but he guaran-fuckin-teed he could double my money. When I told him I was a poor student and had no money, he asked me if I knew anyone that did. He had no front teeth and he said his old lady was going to kick him out if he didn't come up with some money. He had a bad habit of picking his nose and eating it when he thought I wasn't look-ing. When we parted ways he gave me his phone # and told me to keep in touch. When I got home I took an extra long shower just in case whatever he had was contagious. Another time an old bag tried to pick me up. I think she was only in her thirties, but she looked like she was in her sixties. She smiled at me with dark and decayed teeth and asked me if I wanted a blow job. I practically barfed right there. I politely declined her offer and proceeded to ignore her for the rest of the trip.

* * *

Undoubtably my most interesting patient, Hans, was a Prus-sian in his early fifties.He was tall and handsome with mes-merizing green eyes. His official occupation was bee-keeper. His unofficial career was naturopath, whose work consisted of changing and refining energy flow in unhealthy people.

His personal views were unusual to say the least. Apparently there were two types of people in this world.-real man and repli-cated man. Only real man had souls. There weren't enough souls to go around for all the people that were born. The unfortunate man who was born without a soul was a replicated man, and by nature they were evil. Hans had a sure fire way to test a person's authenticity. It was called a biotensor. It looked like a foot long coat hangar with a weird little metal ball on the end.

His test involved touching you with one hand while he tightly held his biotensor in his other hand. If the little ball on the end bobbed up and down you had a soul. If it swayed sideways you were a replicated man.

He tested me on our first appointment and I guess I passed. He said that we were actually creatures of energy trapped inside human bodies. He believed that the satellites that were in high orbit above us, were transmitting strong energy fields that were manipulating us. There was a group of men in Switzerland that controlled the world in this way. Hans had a way of neutralizing the effects of these energy fields.

As a naturopath he was very successful. He had a devout following that was based on word of mouth. He didn't claim to cure cancer but he had several patients who were deemed palliative by modern medicine who were still living years after they were officially supposed to be dead. People even drove hundreds of miles to see him.

Before we used any material in his mouth he first needed to test it with his biotensor. He used his biotensor and a periodic table of the elements. He placed one finger on the filling material and then placed another finger from that same hand on the periodic table of the elements, on the symbol for the material he was testing. He'd ask me,"Is there barium in this material?" I'd say, "No."He put one finger on the filling material and another on the symbol for barium, Ba, and sure enough his little biotensor went back and forth sideways. It was safe. There was no barium in the sample. He proceeded through the periodic table and by the time we were done, the sample was declared safe. It was free of any undesirable materials. Amalgam was considered toxic and so were light cured white fillings. White fillings that were chemically cured were the only safe filling material that he would allow in his mouth. He said that the energy from the light cure filling gave the material too much energy spin that was harmful to the oral cavity. His testing was so bizarre that I wanted to laugh but Hans was so serious that I didn't dare laugh.

It didn't take long to finish his fillings because we could only use the one type of filling material. After we were all done he suggested that I come to his office and have my energy fields adjusted. I agreed because I was curious and I didn't want to hurt his feelings.

A couple of weeks later I found myself lying on my back on a large leather lounger. He had attached a couple of electrodes to my bare chest. The electrodes were taped on and they were connected by thin thread to an empty Campbell's soup can. He stood behind the can and asked me questions. On the wall above me was a huge picture of Martin Luther King, the German theologian. His questions started harmlessly enough, "Did I want to be a dentist?" "Yes." "Did I like dental school?" "No, " "Did I have a girl friend?" "Yes" "Did I love her?" "yes" "Was I happy?" I had to think about that one for a while before I said, "No"

Next thing I knew I was sobbing like a baby. I couldn't stop. My tears were just streaming down and I was crying so hard I could barely catch my breath. He let me cry for a good long time and then he asked a few more harmless questions and he said he was done. He told me not to be embarrassed and that the treatment went very well, He further told me that my waste products (pee and poo) would smell funny for the next couple of days. He was right, they did..

To this day I have no idea what happened that day but for the next few weeks I felt lighter in my steps. It was hard to describe but   I felt better. The world seemed like a happier place and even dental school wasn't as bad..

By shear bad luck Paul ended up with two of the worst patients in all of fourth year. Carla was a Macedonian woman in her late fifties. She always wore black and she always had a babushka on. She was a nice enough lady. Her problem was that she was a moaner, a groaner, a crier and a screamer. It didn't matter what Paul did, from the moment he put the rubber dam on until he took it off Carla made noise. A lot of noise. It sounded like he was torturing her. He would ask her if it hurt and she always said no. One of our instructors got tired of her constant non-verbal tirade and he even suggested that she go else where to have her dental work finished.

It definitely was disruptive to the whole clinic. We all learned not to book our patients when Carla was in because of the so-called" Carla phenomenon." The phenomenon was that whenever Carla was acting up by moaning, groaning and screaming, we needed to use at least twice as much freezing to keep our patients comfortable. Carla put everybody on edge.

Every time Carla walked out of the clinic she did the same thing. She held her lower jaw in her hands and she moaned, like she had just been in a car accident. We all felt sorry for Paul.

Paul's other nightmare patient was George. George owned a diner downtown and he was a burly, almost-bald man in his early forties. The problem with George was that he was a whiner and complainer. Paul took too long. The filling Paul did last time didn't feel right. Paul had bad breath. George didn't like the male instructors. Why did Paul always have to use the rubber dam? How come Paul had to use so much freezing? How come it took so long for the freezing to come out? George drove Paul crazy. One day Paul finally asked him why he bothered coming to the clinic if it was so bad. George said, "At my regular dentist it costs too much and I never get a chance to complain."

Paul's last clinical requirement to complete on George was a gold inlay. It took Paul over two hours to convince George that the gold inlay was a good idea. The only reason George agreed to it in the end was because Paul offered to do it for free even though the gold was worth over a hundred and fifty dollars.

When Paul went to try in the inlay he discovered he had a major problem. There was a two- to three-millimeter gap between the inlay and the tooth. It would have been an automatic failure. He sent the complaining George home (Why do we need another appointment?) and we brain-stormed the problem. We came up with an elegant but unethical solution. There were two factors. Firstly, how could we possibly get this by one of our eagle-eyed instructors and secondly, how could we fake the x-ray to make it look like the inlay actually fit.

The first problem we solved by using Dr Jan. He was a first rate researcher and lecturer but he hadn't done any wet finger dentistry for at least a decade. He made us put the hand mirror in the patient's mouth and he never, ever picked up an excavator to check things.

The x-ray problem was taken care of by tilting the x-ray head by fifty degrees to the right angle. From the skewed angle there was no gap evident and it appeared that the inlay fit precisely.

The plan worked perfectly. Paul showed Dr Jan the x-ray and Dr Jan looked inside of George's mouth for about three seconds before he said, " "Good job." Paul was ecstatic. George walked out of the clinic not knowing that recurrent decay was already starting under the open margins of the inlay. I think we were all kind of amazed that Paul got away with it. But we all agreed on one thing. It couldn't happen to a more deserving patient.

* * *

Our final exams took place right after our March break. They were actually our national dental examining board exams. Passing these exams would allow us to practice dentistry anywhere in Canada. In total we had nine exams.

Although I had the whole week off to study for the exams, I was having a hard time. I wasn't alone. Almost everyone I knew was having problems studying. I think we had all reached a saturation point. We just didn't care anymore. We'd been through so much already that these last exams seemed merely a formality. We'd never heard of any students failing the board exams. There were also about a thousand old board exams that we studied from. And the questions were amazingly easy. All the exams were in a simple multiple- choice format. So when it came time to do the exams, nobody seemed too concerned about them. I still needed to take sleeping pills at night time to get to sleep.

I'd read somewhere that if you chewed gum during an exam, your marks would be higher. So I chewed gum like a fiend. There were no real surprises since about seventy percent of the exam questions were word-for-word identical to the old exams we were using to study from. The whole thing just seemed like another stupid, meaningless exercise we had to endure to graduate. When the week of exams was over, it felt anticlimactic. I didn't even go out at the end to celebrate. Instead I went to a movie with Nancy and afterwards we talked about the future. I wanted to practice in my home town and she wanted to nurse in one of the larger cities that had teaching hospitals. We had reached an impasse. I knew that she wouldn't come with me unless I proposed to her. And I wasn't ready for marriage yet. I did know that I was in love with her. During the last two years of dental school she was my rock. I didn't know what I would do without her.

Just before March break I had gone for an interview with three dentists who owned a couple of mall clinics. It appeared to be the only place that was hiring in my home town. All three dentists were in their early forties, and they seemed to be quite successful. Dr Jim had a problem making eye-contact. The whole time I talked to him, he was looking at the ceiling behind me. Dr Mike had a fake eye and at first I thought he was cross-eyed. I wasn't sure which eye I should look into.Dr Gord looked normal. I directed most of my questions to him. He was only about five feet tall and he seemed to suffer from small man complex. He was obviously the leader of the three and the other two constantly deferred to him, "So why do you want to work for us?" Gord asked. I felt like saying."because you're the only guys in town who're hiring." I replied, "I have a lot of friends and relatives in the city who are planning to see me as patients and your locations are perfect, they're very central and easy to get to." Gord continued, " I hope you don't mind working nights and weekends?" "I'm not a morning person so nights are perfect for me, and weekends are no big deal,it's not like I have kids or a wife to worry about," I answered. They seemed particularly happy with that reply. I could almost see them rubbing their hands together and counting the money. They asked me if I had any hobbies. "I'm into photography, (I hadn't taken any pictures in at least a year), fishing, (I hadn't fished for at least five years), skiing, (I hadn't skied in over four years) squash(I hadn't played in over six years), painting (all I've ever painted was walls), reading (mostly science fiction which I didn't mention)and writing. They seemed impressed.

Gord asked, "What's your favorite medium for painting." I didn't have a clue what to say. I stammered out, "You know, the same as the old masters." "Ah, I find oils kind of tricky. I much prefer acrylics. Have you tried acrylics?" "Yeah, I didn't have much luck with acrylics, I find the oils much easier to work with " I answered. And with that my interview was over. Gord said, "We need to talk this over together, but we'll let you know by the end of the week. We still have a few other dentists to interview (they didn't) I stood up and shook each of their hands with one erg short of a bone crusher grip. I thanked them for their time and said I was hoping to be working with them in the future. I knew I had the job by the way they were acting. Dr Jim had actually made eye contact with me, Dr Mike had focused his one good eye right on me and Dr Gord shook my hand with an even stronger grip than mine. When they called me a week later my roommate Ed answered the phone the first time. Ed hung up on them before I had a chance to come to the phone. When they phoned two minutes later I answered the phone. I could smell their desperation. It was Dr Gord on the phone."Ken, how are you? I hope you're sitting down, because you have the job." All I had to do was pass all my exams and graduate. We talked about a starting time and I thanked him profusely.Just the day before I had finished my last exam. Now I actually had a job, I couldn't believe it.

When I got off the phone I was absolutely overjoyed. I called Nancy to let her know. She was happy for me but I could read the slight diffusion in her tone of voice. I asked her to come over and help me celebrate. We went out for dinner to a fifties style diner and drank a whole bottle of mateus. When we got home we were each a little drunk and I ended up passing out on her. The next morning we both had hangovers. She told me then that she had to go to a big city hospital for the sake of her career. When I told her that her career wasn't as important as mine I knew I'd made a mistake as soon as the words were out of my mouth. I don't think I'd ever seen her so angry. I quickly back pedaled and apologized for my comment, but the damage was done. I told her that I wanted to marry her. I didn't know what else to say. I guess it was the right thing because two minutes later we were in the bedroom making everything right again. Nancy always made me feel safe and I didn't want to lose that security.

When Nancy told me that she was going to the Bahamas with three of her nursing friends to celebrate her graduation I was freaked out. I was so scared she was going to meet some super-rich, super-handsome dude down there, that I tried to talk her out of it. When I told her my fears she just laughed, she said she loved me and that I had nothing to worry about. But then I started thinking. If she can go on a graduation trip why can't I?

I talked it over with my parents and they thought a trip would be a great graduation present for me. Of my friends only Paul was able to afford it. We went to a travel agent and she booked us week-long trip to Jamaica, leaving two days after our graduation date. Now I had to graduate. And I had something really exciting to look forward to as well.

Before I was officially done fourth year I had one last clinical requirement to fulfil. I had cemented a porcelain fused to metal crown on Gary the week before, but the instructor hadn't given me credit for it, since we ran out of time. I knew that it would only take about ten minutes to get the crown checked off.

The only problem was that I couldn't find Gary. I phoned his home and his mother didn't know where he was. Gary was a thirty-year-old unemployed slacker who lived in the basement of his mom's house. His great claim to fame in his life was that he'd won twenty-five thousand dollars with a scratch and win ticket when he was sixteen. He couldn't cash it himself so he had his brother who was nineteen cash it for him. He didn't see his brother for five months after he'd cashed the ticket and by that time the money was all gone. So what did Gary do? He just bought more and more scratch and win tickets. But he never again hit it big.

I looked up Gary's brother's number in the phone book and called him. It turns out Gary and his brother hadn't talked in ten years. His brother had no idea where Gary was. I was starting to panic. If I didn't get Gary's crown checked off I wasn't going to graduate unless I did a whole new crown on another patient.

I finally remembered that Gary had a girlfriend that worked at the Dollar Store at the nearby mall and her name was Vanessa. I looked up the number for the store and called. I asked for Vanessa.After what seemed like an eternity on hold Vanessa came on line and answered. "Yeah this is Vanessa, how may I help you?" "Hi Vanessa, this is Gary's dentist. I'm trying to find him to set up our next appointment. Do you know where he is? She replied, "Oh, he's gone camping." I asked her,"Do you know where he's camping or when he's going to come back?"

"Uh... I don't know, ..like Gary and I like broke up... last month. Why don't you call his mother? She should know where he's at." I thanked the lovely Vanessa for her time and started to panic in earnest. And. then I remembered. Gary used to talk about going camping. He liked to go camping and fishing by the reservoir north of town. I remembered because he used to brag about all the fish he caught.

On a long shot I decided to drive out to the reservoir. If I was right I was laughing. If I was wrong at least I'd gone for a nice drive. After a half hour I was there but I had no idea where to look. And then I remembered that he'd said the best fishing was right under the highway bridge. I parked my car on the highway bridge and walked down the steep slope to get to the river. I looked both upstream and downstream and thought I saw a tent about a kilometer away right underneath the dam. It was hard to see because of the dense undergrowth.

There was a fairly-well-traveled path running adjacent to the river towards the dam. I started walking towards the dam. About a hundred yards along the path I heard what sounded like a gunshot. Suddenly a scruffy looking kid in his late teens came running down the path in my direction. Just before he was about to pass me I asked if he knew Gary C.

The ridiculousness of the situation dawned on me. Here I was in the middle of nowhere.

I'd just heard a gunshot and I'm asking an obviously delin-quent teen who should be in school if he knew a sub-mental cretin named Gary. The kid stopped running and looked at me as if he'd seen a ghost."Are you a cop?"he stammered. Maybe I was in the right place. "No I'm not a cop,I'm Gary's dentist " I said. The young man seemed obviously relieved. "Oh Gary's over there by the tent." I felt like getting on my hands and knees and kissing this kid's feet. I was in shock. I'd found Gary.

I hurried further down the path and eventually I came to a clearing about a hundred feet from the tent. Sure enough there was Gary. He had a very real-looking gun in his hands and he was pointing it right at me. My first thought was,"I guess he didn't like the crown" I I walked closer until I was about thirty feet away from him. He was still pointing the gun right at me. For a second I saw his pupils constrict and I thought I was a goner. "Gary, don't you recognize me? I'm your dentist." He put his gun down and said,"Hi!" Gary didn't seem to be finding it strange that his dentist was here at his secret camping spot. Before he had a chance to fire his handful of neurons together I said, "Boy am I glad to see you. I need you to come to the clinic tomorrow at two for a ten minute appointment, It's very important."

I think for a moment Gary entertained the idea of raising his gun up and shooting me. I wasn't at the clinic, I was in his domain. Gary looked down at his feet and said rather meekly,"I'll be there."

The next day Gary was fifteen minutes late for his appointment but he showed up. It seemed the longest fifteen minutes of my life. I was determined that if he didn't show I was going to go back to the reservoir and haul his sorry ass right to the clinic myself. When Gary trudged into the clinic at two fifteen I was ready. I brought him into my cubicle and thanked him for showing up. He was wearing the same clothes from yesterday and smelled like ass and campfire.

Dr Thomsky checked off the crown ten minutes later. The moment Dr Thomsky scrawled his signature across my mark card I felt as if the weight of the world had been lifted from my shoulders. I wanted to SCREAM at the top of my lungs. But still I was wary, it seemed too easy. I knew I wouldn't truly relax until I walked across the stage at graduation with that degree in my hand. It was still in their power to do anything. If they approached me right before I was to walk across the stage and asked me to make love to nurse Watson I would have done it. Jump through a hula hoop. No problem-how high?

Graduation was still three weeks away. Two days later the faculty posted a list. On that list was the name of every student who had fulfilled the clinical and academic requirements to graduate.

Some of the students had a star beside their name. The star denoted that the student had outstanding work. My name was on the list , but I didn't have a star beside my name. I was a little disappointed, I thought my work was pretty good"Why didn't I end up with outstanding work?And when I checked the names it didn't make any sense. The weaker students had stars besides their names, not the better students. It didn't make any sense.

It wasn't until the next day that I realized the true meaning of the stars. Outstanding meant that the students still had clinical work to finish before they could graduate. I couldn't believe how stupid I was. Now I was glad I had no star beside my name.

As far as finishing our clinical requirements were concerned, the school was totally inflexible. You either had enough credits or you didn't That was why I had to hunt and track down Gary. Dave W. had a similar experience. He'd finished a three-unit bridge on a patient. All he had to do was cement the bridge permanently and have it checked off. Unfortunately the temporary bridge that Dave had placed, looked so good that his patient didn't want to come back. The bridge went right from the front, top, central incisor to the canine tooth. Being right at the front of the mouth you couldn't miss it. The instructors had always warned us never to make a temporary look too good, or there was a chance your patient wouldn't come back. Instead of heeding their advice Dave had spent hours making the temporary bridge look beautiful.

The temporary bridge was made of a plastic that was no where as strong as the permanent porcelain fused to metal bridge. The plastic could last for days or years. Dave was despondent. He phoned and phoned his patient, leaving messages that were sounding more and more desperate. The patient never called Dave back and after five days Dave was sinking into hopeless despair. Eventually Dave drove to his patient's house and rang the front doorbell. Nobody was home. Dave ended up staking out his patient's house for the next two days. When his patient walked up to his front door, Dave walked over and said, "Hi." His patient stared in disbelief and said,"Hey man, What are you doing here?" Dave replied,"The dental school sent me to find you and make sure you're okay. They're very worried that your temporary bridge may break at any time, leaving you in a lot of pain. They need you back at the clinic to get your permanent bridge cemented." The patient looked confused. He said,"Like I thought this was the permanent bridge. I thought we were all done. That's why I didn't return your calls. It didn't make no sense to me." Ignoring the double negative Dave replied," No, you only have the really cheap temporary right now. We still need to cement the expensive permanent bridge, that you've already paid for." His patient whined," What do you mean expensive? I already paid six hundred dollars. Are you like trying to rip me off?"

Dave replied,"No you don't understand. You've already paid for the permanent bridge. We just need to cement it. Can you come with me, right now to the clinic?" The patient answered, "Right now, man. I'm really busy, but like I don't want to get ripped off. Can I get like a ride with you, to like the clinic?

Dave drove him back to the clinic, removed his temporary bridge and finally cemented the permanent bridge, all in the same day. Dave was thrilled. He too was finished his clinical requirements.

That night Dave and I went to a party that one of the Army guys was having to celebrate graduation. Almost all the obnoxious people in my class were there. Dave and I felt pretty uncomfortable. After a few drinks most of the people seemed to mellow out. After a few drinks I just got more uncomfortable. The conversations were devoted to how much money everyone was going to make, and what kind of great cars everyone was going to drive. Dave and I felt invisible. Paul, Dan or Vijay weren't there because they still weren't finished all their clinical work.

I tried out a joke." "So what's the difference between a porcupine and a BMW?" I waited before I delivered the punch line. "With the BMW, the pricks are on the inside!" All conversation in the room stopped and everybody just stared at me. And then to my amazement people started to laugh. Suddenly I felt a part of the group rather than an outsider. After a few more drinks I was starting to enjoy myself. These people weren't actually that bad.

Until one of the Army guys got right in my face and started cutting up Marcus. He said, " Yeah what a loser. I sure wouldn't want Marcus working in my mouth. His only patient ever is going to be his mom." I flipped. Without thinking I grabbed him by his collar and tossed him to the ground. I sat on him and was ready to punch when my rage flared out of me. It all happened in about five seconds. He was about my height and weight, but I think he saw something in my eyes that stopped him from retaliating. Being in the Army I'm sure he knew how to kill me in about a hundred different ways.

I got off of him, didn't say a word and walked over to Dave. " Dave, do you mind if we leave now?" I asked. We were out the door ten seconds later.

On the way home Dave and I did a post-party autopsy." What a bunch of materialistic assholes," I began. Dave continued,-"They're never going to be happy. There's always going to be somebody who has more toys and more, bigger possessions than they have." I winked at Dave and said, "Aren't you glad we're not like that? And remember,grasshopper, the happy man is the one who's happy with what he has." Dave sighed and said, "Fuck you, Ken." It was a good night.

Now that graduation was imminent it was time to reflect on the dental school experience. Overall it was depressing, demoralizing and dehumanizing. In all four years there was practically no positive feedback. The instructors, for the most part, were cruel and sadistic. If it wasn't for our black sense of humor and camaraderie I don't think I would have survived.

We were taught such a large volume of material that we never really had a chance to figure out what we weren't taught. But the "not taught" list was extensive. We weren't taught anything useful in orthodontics, except that when teeth weren't straight we were to refer to an orthodontist. In oral surgery we only had a chance to take out a few teeth, so we had practically no experience in extractions. We weren't even taught enough to know when to refer to an oral surgeon or when to attempt an extraction by ourselves.

We only completed one full denture on a patient in four years. How could we be expected to provide full denture treatment with so little experience?-Why were we taught to do so many silver fillings when there were a lot of practicing dentists who had entire " no silver filling practices." The root canal technique that we were taught was practically never used in private practice anymore. We were taught almost nothing about the business of dentistry. The first associate agreement I ever saw was the one I signed. We were as lambs to the slaughter of the real world .

What were we supposed to do when a patient adamantly refused our treatment recommendation and instead wanted us to provide a service that we knew would fail? What about the patient who insisted that the filling you put in two weeks ago had fallen out, when in fact, the filling you had done was fine and instead it was the filling beside their new filling, that had fallen out. No matter what you said the patient didn't believe you and demanded that you do the filling for free.

How about the patient who came in and said he had a bad tooth, that he wanted you to hock it out. On x-ray the roots were right into the sinus and you knew the extraction should be done by an oral surgeon. But the patient insisted you do it right there and right then "cuz he didn't have the money to see no specialist."

How were we expected to convince a patient to get a six thousand dollar bridge when we weren't even sure if we could do it properly? We learned next to nothing about cosmetic dentistry, but in the real world everyone was talking cosmetic dentistry. We weren't taught anything about tooth bleaching.

What we actually did learn was the technical know-how of fixing a decayed tooth, and that was about it. We were taught so much, yet we knew so little.

Walking across the stage at Convocation was almost anti-climactic, It was just one more exercise. Hear your name, walk to the front of the stage, perform a little bow, shake hands with your right hand, grab your degree with your left hand and walk across the stage.

It all happened so fast. On stage were all of our profs. Every university had a different color robe and it looked like Mardi Gras with all the colors and weird hats. It would have been funny if it wasn't so damned serious. I remembered my previous Convocation, when I had graduated from Chemistry. That was a long, laborious, drawn-out affair. One of the graduating students was named Kitty Chow. When I heard that I couldn't stop laughing. I spent most of the ninety-minute ceremony trying to suppress my laughter.

This time around it was a much smaller affair. The whole ceremony was for our graduating class only. When each of us went up to receive our degree the audience clapped. I was shocked that when it was my turn I seemed to get the loudest applause of all. Most of the clapping came from my fellow students- I had no idea I was so popular.

After the ceremony there was a small reception for all graduates and their families outside the Convocation hall.- I didn't want to go. I just wanted to get as far away from the dental school as I could. Unfortunately to get from the Convocation hall to the parking lot you had to pass right through the reception area. I couldn't avoid it. With my head down and the far end of the reception area my goal I waded through the throngs of people. We were all high fiving each other when I walked right into Dr Moore.

I didn't realize what a short man he was until that moment when we stood face to face, his eyes at about the level of my Adam's apple."Congratulations, Ken, now that you've graduated you can call me Allan,"he whined. My mind raced. I thought about four years of my life irrevocably lost-, the stress, the agony. And then I looked at this pee-wee sized self-styled dictator in front of me.

I said,"-Thanks,Allan, but you can call me Dr Spaldane." I brushed past him, impervious to the startled look on his face, high fives landing on my palms like the drums of an anthem. I stepped on to the pavement of the parking lot, not even looking back once.

LaVergne, TN USA
29 December 2010
210463LV00004B/93/P